# Single & Gifted

Making the **most** of your singleness

**by Jeffrey Brown**

**Editor:**
Dr David Marshall, BA, PhD

**Medical Editor:**
Dr Eileen Baildam, MD, DCH, MRCGP, FRCP, FRCPCH

**Consulting Editors:**
Karen Holford, MA, Family Counsellor
Isobel Webster, MA

**Design:**
Lee Gallaher



Printed in Thailand for
AUTUMN HOUSE, Grantham, Lincs., England.

ISBN 1-873796-91-9

Bible translations used:
The Living Bible, unless otherwise stated.
Other translations (abbreviated):
**JBP** – J. B. Phillips
**KJV** – King James Version
**NEB** – New English Bible
**NKJV** – New King James Version

Reprinted 2003 and 2005

# Single & Gifted

Making the **most** of your singleness

# This book is dedicated to:

**My praying church families in:** Apple Creek and Hands of Glory, Toronto; Southampton, Bermuda; Bauer and Niles, Michigan; Manchester, Birmingham, Reading, Leeds, Bradford, Barnsley, Oldham, Wolverhampton, and London, UK; Kingsboro Temple, New York; New Hope, Atlanta; and Operation ReachBack, Washington D.C.

**My caring institutions:** Harper Bell School; Newbold School; Crawford Academy; John Loughborough School; Newbold College; Relate Reading; Oakwood College; Collonges-sous-Saleve; Kingsway College; Andrews University and Loma Linda University.

**My supportive colleagues and their families:** Lucia Hall; Esmie Branner, Trace White; Wendell Phipps; Ursula Lewis; Miriam Francis; Audley Allen; Eric Tappenden; Pastors Theodore Stewart, Michael Anderson, Halsey Peat, Hymers Wilson, Richard Holder, Cyril Millett, Borbor Gibson, Cyril Sweeney, Michael Simpson, Bruce Flynn, Glendon Cross, Ian Sweeney, Don McPhaull, Alvin Kibble, Wayne Martin, Nigel David, Garry Gordon, Ray Allen, Gifford Rhamie, Everett Picart, Steve Palmer, Clyde Moore, Moses Msimanga, Matthew Bediako, Jeff Shiplett, Gregory St. Ange, Frank Dell'Erba, Arthur Branner, Errol Nembhard, Harold Johnson, Orville Woolford, Winsley Hector, Stennett Ross, Michael Mannix, Keith Morris and Fanny Anderson-Chan, Drs Calvin Rock, Albert Waite, Norman Miles, Clinton Valley, Leslie Pollard, Walter Pearson, Nerval Myrie, Ron Smith, Elsie Jackson, Alonzo Smith, Herbert Thompson, Andrea Luxton, Patrick Herbert, Richard DeLisser, Hyveth Williams, Lisa Beardsley, Errol Lawrence and Haskell Edwards.

**My faithful friends:** Karl and Denise Marshalleck-Smith; Sheena Sadler; Yolanda White; Dessaline Waldron; Paula Webber; Dr Marquita Rand; Judith Hall; Isaac and Jacqueline Collie; Jude and Dr Merle Roberts; Alvin and Babita Jackson; Stafford and Lisa Byers; Bob and Patrice Smith; Malcolm and Shirlene Nisbett; Kareena Elliston; Angeline Joseph; Madge, Avril-May, Dr Melanie and Dr Jeffrey Edwards; Dr Dahlia Pottinger; Susanne Kirlew; Earl and Dawn Edwards; Joseph and Maria Ratteray; Devie Phipps; Del Stewart; Sophia and Henry Rose; Carmen Carter-McLeary; Keith Hill; Marcia Dormus; Theresa Saber; Ken and Hyacinth Callum; Bridget Banton; Charles and Susan Kellen; Dr David and Paulette Burt; Dave and Juliette Knight; Dana Bassett; Michelle Raynor; and Deborah Harvey.

**My beloved family:** Ivy Powell; Carmen Brown; Dr Maurice and Launa Brown; the Browns: Eric, Anne, Michael, and Jacynth, the Prices, Gillespies, Stewarts, Mings, Butlers, and Daleys, in England and Jamaica; the Roberts in the USA and Canada. Myrtle McMahon; Isabelle McMahon; Charles McMahon; the McMahons: Donald, Alvin, and Wayne, the Darrells in Bermuda, Bahamas, USA and Canada.

**Our adopted mothers:** Eleanor (and Francis) Raab, and Vera (and Dawn) Forrest.

**My devoted wife:** Pattiejean, and our loving children; Kristle and Jamel.

**Our loving Saviour:** Jesus.

# Single & Gifted

Making the **most** of your singleness

## About the author

**Dr Jeffrey Brown**, with his wife Pattiejean, conducts relationship seminars for singles. He has pastoral and teaching experience, and has taught Family Life courses at undergraduate and graduate levels. He has lectured on the 'Single and Gifted' theme in Africa, North America and Britain.

Dr Brown's PhD comes from Andrews University in Michigan. He is an ordained minister and a qualified counsellor.

Single & **Gifted**

# Contents

Make the **most** of your singleness . . .

# Chapter 1

# Waiting to exhale

Dear Dr Brown

I am having a hard time dealing with my anger towards the guy I was engaged to. I don't feel guilty, because I don't like him. I know this is OK. I just don't know what to do with all my bad feelings towards him. Being treated so badly by him has made me scared to open up to other guys – which I think is terrible because it is only by revealing yourself to someone that you truly discover who you are and, in turn, they share what makes them who they are. I need to be willing to take chances.

I believe that the best person for me to consult concerning this is God, and I do. But I also feel like I need to talk to someone else. Being here, so far away from my family and close friends, has made this healing process even harder. Sometimes I feel so alone. I just don't think I can work through all my pain and anger alone.

Jennifer
(names have been changed throughout)

## All in the same boat

Some years ago a film came out that caused a stir among men and women, particularly single men and women. It was called *Waiting to Exhale*. Some thought the film portrayed all men as dogs, men who treat women badly and then toss them aside. The writer says this was not her purpose.

The film was based on the best-selling book of the same title, written by prolific African-American female author, Terry McMillan. *Waiting to Exhale* was inspired by McMillan's personal experiences as she moved through unfulfilling and sometimes explosive relationships over the years. *Ebony* magazine wrote: 'She realized that many of her friends were in

the same boat: "educated, smart, attractive, and alone."'

That's the situation of many of us today: educated, smart, attractive – and alone. We're all in the same boat. Otis Redding says we're 'sitting on the dock of the bay, watching the tide roll away, sitting on the dock of the bay, wasting time'. Life is passing us by. Unable to function because there's no partner on our arm. Holding our breath until we find someone to hold our hand. Waiting to exhale. The question is, isn't there more to life than this?

## Singleness shipwreck?

Is singleness a tragic wreck or a tremendous resource? Is singleness helplessness or hopefulness? Is singleness full of problems or full of promise? There seems to be a force propelling us all into a ship called marriage and, even when we see the name *Titanic* written on the ship, we still can't wait to jump on board.

Marrieds don't help by saying, 'What's a nice person like you still doing single?' Still others attempt to be sympathetic by saying, 'Don't worry, there's nothing wrong with being single.' Our mentality seems to be shaped more by Hollywood than the Holy Word.

## Holy Word or Hollywood?

Psychologist Dr Aric Sigman is the author of *New? Improved?* He had a programme on BBC Radio entitled *God on the Couch* and he states, 'Hollywood constantly needs change and permutations of themes to survive. The people in charge of the media usually lead pretty bizarre lives themselves. The decisions they make based on their own perceptions of "reality" have nothing to do with the reality of the woman at home on a Paisley council estate looking after her kid. Yet what they decide has a huge amount of influence.'

## Good luck?

Some time ago a cartoon appeared in a national newspaper of a frustrated motorist trying to cross a busy intersection. Horns were honking, engines were revving, tempers were flaring, and arms were waving. The poor man looked hope-

fully towards the traffic signal for him to cross and he couldn't believe his eyes. The signal didn't say, 'Walk.' It didn't say, 'Don't Walk.' Instead it said, 'Good Luck.'

The Bible talks about people, so-called guides, whose message, when all is said and done, is just, 'Good luck.' The Bible calls them 'broken cisterns'.

## Broken cisterns

Hollywood has not improved on the Holy Word. In fact, we have been terribly let down by the so-called 'experts'. The Bible says, 'My people have committed two evils; they have forsaken me the fountain of living waters, and hewed them out cisterns, broken cisterns, that can hold no water' (Jeremiah 2:13, KJV). If the truth be told, so many of the counsels that we hear today are from people whose own lives are a mess – broken cisterns, broken water pots that can hold no water. Listen to some of these broken cisterns.

Ronald Mazur wrote – in his book *Commonsense Sex* – that the problem we face in relationships is never 'to bed or not to bed' but 'to become or not to become'. Mazur would have us believe that premarital sex is a key element of personal growth. He says, 'Today chastity means acting with integrity. Either a virgin or a non-virgin ought to be chaste – this is the essence of the single standard of sexual behaviour – so that if the path of

The wisdom of man and the wisdom of God are not the same.

"going all the way" is chosen, we will not end in a dark pit of remorse, but will discover a highlight in the fascinating journey of becoming.'

The O'Neills wrote the book *Open Marriage*, advising couples to open themselves up to other couples – if you had a secure relationship, you could only benefit by someone else's husband admiring your wife and someone else's wife being attentive to your husband.

David Sammons, a divorced minister living with his girlfriend, wrote a book called *The Marriage Option*. He advocated alternative lifestyles such as those suggested by renowned sociologist Margaret Mead, saying:

'Margaret Mead has suggested that rather than do away with marriage conceived of as primarily a one-to-one relationship, we should break it up into a series, since the needs we have as spouses vary as we progress through life. One's first marriage would be for learning about sex and romance. In between one's early and late marriages would be marriage for the conception of children and the raising of families. Finally, late in life would come marriage for companionship.'

Dr Mead was not reluctant to follow out at least part of this model in her own life.

Then there's the famous Fritz Perls. Dr Fritz Perls' credo hangs on the waiting room walls of hundreds of psychotherapists, presumably to help the love lives of their patients:

'I do my thing, and you do your thing.
I am not in this world to live up to
your expectations.
And you are not in this world to live
up to mine.
You are you and I am I,
And if by chance we find each other,
it's beautiful.
If not, it can't be helped.'

Alan Loy McGinnis, in *The Romance Factor,* addresses the philosophy of Fritz Perls: 'Such an idiosyncratic way of living has its attractions, but adherents of that philosophy should at least refrain from marrying and bearing children. Perls' wife and two children, whom he abandoned, did not feel that they benefited from his egocentrism.'

## Dressed-up living, messed-up lives

These so-called experts have promised us fulfilment and growth and all we've got from them are confused children, problem parents, messed-up marrieds and sorry singles. Ronald Clapp wrote an article in *Christianity Today* in which he attests that the advertising industry, movies, novels, and television shows have realized their financial aspirations through their misuse of the word love. Taking advantage of the word love, so they get the money and we get the misery. He called his article, 'What Hollywood doesn't know about romantic love.' So I say, move over Hollywood, let's give God's Holy Word a chance!

## Upside-down values

You don't have to read the Bible for very long to discover that it turns many of our modern values upside down. It says you get by giving (Luke 6:38), you multiply by dividing (Mark 6:41-44), you win by losing (Luke 9:24) and you live by dying (John 12:24, 25). The Bible says give ten per cent of your salary to God's work and you'll discover that nine-tenths goes further than ten tenths (Malachi 3:8-11)! Rest on the Sabbath and you'll discover you can do more in six days than you could in seven (Exodus 20:8-11)!

So with relationships, the Bible turns singleness on its head. It is not just tolerated – it is advocated! Look what the apostle Paul says: 'I wish everyone could get along without marrying, just as I do. But we are not all the same. God gives some the gift of a husband or wife, and others he gives the gift of being able to stay happily unmarried' (1 Corinthians 7:7). You are single – and gifted, too.

## Freedom

One of the most coveted values in the world today is freedom. Many men brag about their freedom as if it's something they are afraid will be taken away from them once they are married. Hollywood even wants women to envy and emulate the so-called freedom that men have, in sex and violence.

Psychologist Dr Aric Sigman says, 'Mimicking male behaviour has nothing to do with emancipation or freedom from the constraints of society. I have a young daughter myself and I find the whole thing quite irritating. If she's getting all these false messages about female empowerment through imitating men, it's wrong. Our gender has nothing to show women about freeing themselves. Quite the opposite.'

Quite the opposite. You see, many of us men are not free. Oh, we talk the talk;

> The so-called experts have promised fulfilment and growth and all we've got from them are confused children, problem parents, messed-up marrieds and sorry singles.

but we're not free. Freedom is not the watchword of our lives – it's *fear.* Many men are afraid to *confess*, afraid to *connect*, and afraid to *commit*. They don't want to go to counselling, they don't want to attend marriage enrichment seminars, they don't want to be seen at singles' weekends. They say, 'Those seminars are for people who can't settle down, people who can't find a partner, people with certain problems and since I don't have those problems I don't need to be there.'

Many of us men are afraid to open up, afraid to be vulnerable, afraid to let down our mask, afraid to care, afraid to be shown our weaknesses, afraid to be shown our prejudices, afraid to admit to biases, afraid to laugh at ourselves, afraid to cry with ourselves, and afraid to say, 'I don't have it all together, I need help.'

One of the most coveted values in the world today is freedom.

## Defences

The story is told of a scorpion and a tortoise who were facing a swollen river. The scorpion begged the tortoise to carry him across. 'I can't take you on my back,' the tortoise replied. 'You would sting me.'

'Why would I do that?' the scorpion wanted to know. 'You would be my life raft. If I stung you, we would both drown.'

'Well,' said the tortoise, 'since you put it that way, I guess it'll be all right. Hop on.'

The scorpion climbed on the tortoise's back and they set out across the river. When they were almost to the shore, the scorpion stung the tortoise. As they were both going down, the tortoise turned to the scorpion and said, ruefully, 'Just tell me this – before we drown – why did you do it? I have to know.' The scorpion replied, looking a little regretful, 'What can I tell you? I couldn't help myself. It's my nature.'

Well, perhaps the scorpion may not be able to help himself, *but we can*. We must! That sting was the scorpion's defence and it killed him. There are defences that we put up to show how strong we are, but these defences will destroy us. It's all right to cry! It's all right to break down every now and then, it's all right to need a brother or a sister, it's all right to admit you don't have it all together!

The Bible gives us the source of emancipation. It says, ' "You will know the truth and the truth will set you free." ' It goes on to say, ' "You are slaves of sin, every one of you. And slaves don't have rights, but the Son [of God] has every right there is! So if the Son sets you free, you will indeed be free." ' (John 8:32, 34-36).

Singleness is not about becoming a he-man, it's about becoming His man. It's not about becoming superwoman, but about becoming God's woman. Singleness is about being clean, positive, vibrant, looking up and recognizing that God calls us to aspire and perspire, He calls us to believe and achieve, God summons us not to succumb but to become all that He would have us be.

Happiness in singleness is an attitude of mind. Richard Daly says, in *God's Little Book of Calm*, 'Happiness is a product of the mind, of attitude and thought. It comes from you, not to you. To be happy you must *choose* to be happy.'

Singleness is from God, singleness is biblical, singleness is acceptable, single-

## Single and not satisfied

With my wedding day only weeks away, I want to put in writing some of the feelings I experienced as a single before my happiness with Ken Frazier erases the pain I felt as a single.

Recently, much well-intentioned advice has been given to help Christian singles, but even though I've tried to follow these suggestions, I still felt frustrated as a single.

I felt guilty about not being satisfied as a single, knowing that as Christians we are to be satisfied. I felt guilty about being a sexual being. I did not know how to handle those thoughts.

As a Christian, I am not in the world's system, but live and work there. When others in our office started their 'sex talks', I would get really busy to avoid participating. Being a 28-year-old virgin is not something to brag about to the world. In their eyes, I am a sexual freak.

My problem of being single affected everything in my life – even my relationship to God. One Sunday afternoon, I went to the prayer room in our church and fell down on my hands and knees, weeping before the Lord, asking him, 'Why did you make me?' I need a sense of purpose, and I think singles often feel like they are left on the back burner, *waiting for their time to give themselves to one person* and to start a family.

Donna

## Committed Singleness

In my early twenties, I discovered the secret of fulfilment is in neither singleness nor marriage but in commitment to God's will. When God called me to be a missionary to China, it was difficult to accept the likelihood of remaining single. Yet I had to face reality.

Since we live in an imperfect, sinful world, no one, single or married, has an absolutely ideal situation. One's attitude, not circumstances, determines happiness. Contentment was not found by convincing myself I preferred to be single but rather in praising God for providing resources to make each day meaningful.

The feeling of being loved as a child has continued throughout my life. But there was still a deep hunger for some one person of the opposite sex to love in a special way. Since I was frank enough to admit my feelings of incompleteness, some people tried to help me. Of the men suggested, the only qualifications I could see were that they were male and available. This was hard on my ego.

I was never able to find a satisfactory way to meet my need for physical intimacy. Sometimes I would have given anything for a loving touch. To be touched or caressed by another woman was repulsive to me. God's answer came 'like a bolt out of the blue'.

I received a letter from Dr Herbert J. Miles. He began, 'I have a feeling you will be surprised to receive this letter from me. I'm sure you have heard of the passing of Mrs Miles and know the deep waters I've been passing through.' He went on to say that each time he prayed about whether he should remarry, the name 'Fern Harrington' was given to him.

As a single woman, God has given me a rich, rewarding experience on the mission field, and now the joys of marriage far surpass my fondest dreams.

**Fern Harrington Miles**

ness is OK, singleness is all of these things, but singleness is also *hard* – it's hard! A February 2000 study by Health Canada revealed that single men are 2.3 times as likely to suffer from dementia as married men – and 1.4 times more likely to be institutionalized. Somebody said it is a terrible age in which to be single. And sometimes when you're married you forget how difficult it was to be single. You start mixing with other married couples and you don't invite the singles to dinner any more.

Surrounded by sex, bombarded by beauty, don't fool yourself, singleness is freedom, but it is not easy freedom, it is freedom with limits. And don't think marriage is a lot easier! In fact, when the disciples of Jesus heard the high standard that Jesus placed on faithfulness in marriage, purity in action, word and thought, they cried out, 'If that is how it is, it is better not to marry!' (Matthew 19:10). So singleness is hard and marriage is hard! The apostle Paul would have us know that while we are unmarried there are certain benefits that come our way (1 Corinthians 7:32-34).

'Benefits?' you say. 'There's nothing worse than being single.' I want you to know, there is. There is something worse. Much, much worse. That is, being permanently tied to one with whom you are not fulfilled. It is being in a situation that you can't get out of; where you're giving love but getting nothing in return; where your ability to love and serve God is restricted; where the example being shown to your children is painful and pitiful.

## Time is short

The apostle Paul lived with the idea that the end of the world could come at any moment. For those early Christians, death was just around the corner. People were being martyred for their faith. Paul says, 'The important thing to remember is that our remaining time is very short [and so are our opportunities for doing the Lord's work]' (1 Corinthians 7:29). We would be foolish to believe that these words were only relevant to the particular situation of the church in Corinth in the first century. Fast forward to the twenty-first century.

Dr Johan Candelin, a spokesperson in the United Nations Commission for Human Rights, has dedicated his life to creating an awareness of the plight of Christians who are being persecuted around the world. It is startling to learn that there were more people martyred for their faith in Jesus Christ in the twentieth century than in all the other centuries combined. Is there anything worse than your own death? Yes, there is. It is seeing your spouse suffer and die.

Have you ever read anything about the torturous treatment of Christians under Communist regimes? You will find occasions where the agony was so great they openly declared they wished they had never married. To witness such barbarity against their mates and children was almost unbearable.

Some of you will get the point. In times of crisis, marriage and childbearing can present difficulties. It happened before, and it will happen again. Jesus said, ' "Woe to pregnant women and to those with babies in those days. . . . For there will be persecution such as the world has never before seen in all its history, and will never see again" ' (Matthew 24:19, 21).

You ask, 'So we're not supposed to get married, then?' The Bible says, choose to marry if you wish (1 Corinthians 7:6), but more important than choosing to marry is *choosing to love*. Loving God and loving people. And no one can say where the call to love will take you.

## The call to love

For Mother Teresa, the call to love meant a single life of committed service on the streets of Calcutta. For Dr Martin Luther King, Jun, the call to love meant leading the struggle for civil rights in the United States of America. It was a struggle that ended in his assassination and cost the lives of members of his family. No wonder Deitrich Bonhoeffer, in his book *The Cost of Discipleship*, said, 'When God calls a person, he bids them come and die.'

You say, 'It's better not to love, then!' The call to marry is optional. The call to

### God's plan for my body

'Sexual sin is never right: our bodies were not made for that, but for the Lord, and the Lord wants to fill our bodies with himself. . . . Don't you realize that your bodies are actually parts and members of Christ? So should I take part of Christ and join him to a prostitute? Never! And don't you know that if a man joins himself to a prostitute she becomes a part of him and he becomes a part of her? For God tells us in Scripture that in his sight the two become one person. But if you give yourself to the Lord, you and Christ are joined together as one person. That is why I say you should steer clear of sexual immorality. No other sin affects the body as this one does. When you sin in this way it is against your own body. Haven't you yet learned that your body is the home of the Holy Spirit God gave you, and that he lives within you? Your own body does not belong to you. For God has bought you with a great price. So use every part of your body to give glory back to God, because he owns it.' 1 Corinthians 6:13-20 be single is optional. But the call to love is not. Leo Buscaglia wrote in his book *Living, Loving and Learning*: 'To love is to risk not being loved in return. To hope is to risk pain. And to try is to risk failure. But risk must be taken, because the greatest hazard in life is to risk nothing. Only the person who risks is free.'

If God may not mind *if* you marry, does He mind *who* you marry? In the increasingly diverse societies in which we live, many people are seeking advice about inter-racial marriage.

## Inter-racial marriage

In the United States only a fifth of all inter-racial marriages are Black-White. The remainder, for the most part, are various combinations of Whites, Blacks, Hispanics, Asians, and Native Americans. Surveys show that such couples marry for much the same reason that other couples marry: love and compatibility.

The questions to be asked by an inter-racial couple considering marriage are the same questions to be asked by all couples, whether of a different race or not, whether marrying a disabled person or not, a person with a different religious conviction or not: Will marriage negatively affect what you consider to be God's goal for your life? What about children? What do family and friends think? There are more important considerations than love and compatibility. If you feel God wants you to give some years of service in a developing country, but your partner's interests are elsewhere, you can ask yourself what God may be trying to tell you.

An inter-racial couple may feel that by marrying they are making a statement to society. In a world were racism and discrimination still rear their ugly heads every day, such a statement needs to be made by *all* persons of *all* races, married or single, that, in the words of Acts 17:26, God 'hath

made of one blood all nations of men for to dwell on the face of the earth' (KJV). Ultimately, marriage is not about statements, it's about service. Prepare the best way you can to serve the best way you can.

After a couple have taken counsel and presented their situation to the Lord, let us support their decision *even if it was not our preference*. God didn't spend His time making me *me* just so that you could turn around and make me *you*. Let's give each other a chance, praying for one another rather than preying on one another. Breathe out. In time, the God who made us red and yellow, black and white, the same God will make it plain.

## I just don't fit

One of the crises that face singles is a crisis of identity. Who am I? What am I? Which group do I belong to? Not a child, but not married. In-between. Not at home in either place. I experienced that in-between feeling on my first visit to the West Indies.

Upon my arrival, I decided to act as if I was indeed home. Then a Jamaican lady approached me.

'Young man where are you from?'

'Well, here – Portland – this is my mother's parish.'

'Yes, but you – where are *you* from?'

'Well, I was born in England.'

'Oh, you're an Englishman!'

Upon my return to England, I was in Birmingham when a white lady approached me:

'Young man, where are you from?'

'Well, I'm from here.'

'Yes, but before that.'

'Well, I was born here.'

'Yes, but before that.'

'Lady, you can't get back much further than your birth.'

'Your parents, where are they from?'

'Jamaica.'

'Oh, you're a Jamaican!'

I started to think that the only place I could call home was on an aeroplane, flying somewhere between the two countries. Single person, your testimony may be like those people of faith the Bible talks about: 'They agreed that this earth was not their real home but that they were just strangers visiting down here' (Hebrews 11:13). So make loving God and helping people your focus. Work down here in preparation for life up there.

## What's on your mind?

At a seminar in London, I distributed a survey asking singles what were their biggest concerns. This is how they answered:

**1)** Worship and spiritual growth
**2)** Self-worth and individuality
**3)** Getting older as a single
**4)** Establishing values and priorities
**5)** Finances
**6)** Loneliness
**7)** Communication and listening

Other concerns expressed were:

* Problems of the single parent
* Stigma of divorce
* Singles relationship to the church
* Coping with grief
* Pressure to marry or remarry

Worship and spiritual growth came out on top! The apostle Paul says singles can reach out and touch somebody's life without the distractions that are part and parcel of married life. Melvyn Davis, a youth leader, says, 'Single people have more free time and, in most cases, more money than married couples with children. *The time and money spent raising a family can be spent in service to God.*' It's called *having an undistracted focus.*

## Singleminded

With all the glitter of Hollywood around, it's difficult to have an undistracted focus. But that's what God wants us to have. Paul says, 'I am saying this to help you, not to try to keep you from marrying. I want you to do whatever will help you serve the Lord best, with as few other things as possible to distract your attention from him' (1 Corinthians 7:35). Jesus put it stronger: ' "Anyone who lets himself be distracted from the work I plan for him is not fit for the Kingdom of God" ' (Luke 9:62). Ultimately, the Bible is saying whether we are single or married, each one of us must be *singleminded!* We must not lose sight of our purpose for being.

## Purposeful

A little boy was found crying because he had lost the note his mother gave him for his schoolteacher explaining why he did not have a birth certificate. Wailing aloud, the little boy cried, 'I've lost my excuse for being born!'

You may be a single

Your reason for being born is to brighten up the corner where you are.

parent. You may be single because you've never been married. You may be married to someone, but feel like you're living a single life. You may be single because of death, divorce or delay. But look away from your circumstance for a moment: your reason for being born is to brighten the corner where you are. It's to reach out and touch somebody's hand, it's to make this world a better place, if you can.

It was Soren Kierkegaard who said, 'The door to happiness swings outward.' You are single, but you are gifted – use your gift to bless others. The joyful anticipation of marriage must facilitate, not eclipse, this purpose. And the painful struggle of singleness must illumine, not mar this purpose. That is why God doesn't mind if you marry; He knows just how much you can bear. 'Live life, then, with a due sense of responsibility, not as men [and women] who do not know the meaning of life but as *those who do*' (Ephesians 5:15-17, JBP).

## Solowork on Chapter 1

### It's Why I'm Here

What is the purpose of your life? Og Mandino, in his book *The Greatest Salesman in the World,* came up with ten scrolls which he believed could change your life for the better. In the year which lies ahead of you, meditate on and master one scroll each month.

### The Scroll Marked I

*Today I begin a new life.* I have surrendered my free will to the years of accumulated habits, and the past deeds of my life have already marked out a path which threatens to imprison my future. Today I shed my old skin which has, too long, suffered the bruises of failure and the wounds of mediocrity. I will form good habits and become their slave.

### The Scroll Marked II

*I will greet this day with love in my heart.* I will welcome happiness for it enlarges my heart; yet I will endure sadness for it opens my soul. I will acknowledge rewards for they are my due; yet I will welcome obstacles for they are my challenge. I will love all men for all have qualities to be admired even though they be hidden. Henceforth I will look at all things with love and I shall be born again.

### The Scroll Marked III

*I will persist until I succeed.* I will hear not those who weep and complain, for their disease is contagious. I will avoid despair but if this disease of the mind should infect me then I will work on in despair. Each frown I meet only prepares me for the smile to come. I will be liken to the star which brightens the earth. I must have the night to appreciate the day. I must fail often to succeed only once.

### The Scroll Marked IV

*I am nature's greatest miracle.* I perceive that all my problems, discouragements, and heartaches are, in truth, great opportunities in disguise. Also I will seek constantly to improve my manners and graces, for they are the sugar to which all are attracted. I can achieve far more than I have, and I will, for why should the miracle which produced me end with my birth?

### The Scroll Marked V

*I will live this day as if it is my last.* Should I concern myself over events which I may never witness? Should I torment myself with problems that may never come to pass? Where there are idle mouths I will listen not; where there are idle hands I will linger not; where there are idle bodies I will visit not. Today I shall lift up a friend in need; tomorrow he will no longer cry for help.

### The Scroll Marked VI

*Today I will be master of my emotions.* There will be days when I must constantly struggle against forces which would tear me down. Those such as despair and sadness are simple to recognize, but there are others which approach me with a smile and the hand of friendship and they can also destroy me. Against them, too, I must never relinquish control.

### The Scroll Marked VII

*I will laugh at the world.* Even when confronted by man or deed which offends me so as to bring forth my tears or my curses. Four words I will train myself to say whenever good humour threatens to depart from me. These words, passed down from the ancients, will carry me through every adversity and maintain my life in balance. These four words are: *This too shall pass.*

### The Scroll Marked VIII

*Today I will multiply my value a hundredfold.* I am liken to a grain of wheat with one difference. The wheat cannot choose whether it be fed to swine, ground for bread, or planted to multiply. I have a choice and I will not let my life be fed to swine nor will I let it be ground under the rocks of failure and despair to be broken open and devoured by the will of others.

### The Scroll Marked IX

*I will act now.* I will not avoid the tasks of today and charge them to tomorrow for I know that tomorrow never comes. Let me act now even though my actions may not bring happiness or success for it is better to act and fail than not to act and flounder. Happiness, in truth, may not be the fruit plucked by my action, yet without action all fruit will die on the vine.

### The Scroll Marked X

*I will pray for guidance.* 'O Creator of all things, help me. For this day I go out into the world naked and alone, and without your hand to guide me I will wander far from the path which leads to success and happiness. Expose me to hate so it not be a stranger; yet fill my cup with love to turn strangers into friends. Verily there must be a special place for me. Let me become all you planned for me when my seed was planted and selected by you to sprout in the vineyard of the world. Guide me, God.'

## READ ON!

| Author | Book title | Publisher |
|---|---|---|
| McGinnis, Alan Loy | The Romance Factor | Harper & Row |
| Smith, Wallace Charles | The Church in the Life of the Black Family | Judson Press |
| Swindoll, Charles R. | Singles: Biblical Advice on Staying Single | Multnomah |

# Chapter 2

# Tired of being alone

Dear Dr Brown

Although I respect anybody's choice to be alone, this is not my preference. I would very much like to have the warmth, attention and love of a companion. Sometimes its absence is not an issue for me, but there are moments when my being alone commands my every waking hour and steals some of my sleep. I am aware of my sense of embarrassment as I relay my feelings. I believe this is because the Church on a whole leads young Christian women to believe that they should sit and wait meekly while praying for a partner. However, you're not told what to do with the feelings which emerge and demand your attention and cannot be ignored. Yet you sense that to make mention of these feelings would be deemed undignified.

Recently, my hopes rose as it appeared that I was at last going to escape my loneliness; but an unfaithful friend snatched this opportunity from me. It hurt. It was painful and I became confused. I had prayed about the young man. I knew God was in control because I'd asked Him to take control. Things seemed to be going well, then he was intercepted by a 'friend'. I was disappointed that he could be so easily distracted. I felt rejection by him and betrayal by her.

My hopes of companionship crumbled before me and I was catapulted back into a position of loneliness.

Dr Brown, it often feels like I'm being tortured by God and forced to seek the comfort I need outside of the principles I value. There are moments when I'm driven by Christian principles and, conversely, moments when these principles hold little sway. My intention is to conduct myself as a Christian young lady, but I am very much aware of time peeling away at this determination.

Despite keeping myself busy in social activities and personal development, I still find myself often consumed by loneliness and I am fast losing the ability to cope effectively.

Jeremiah 29:11 tells me that God has great plans for me and I believe this promise, but it doesn't remove the loneliness.

Paulette

## Seeking somebody to share with

'Warm-hearted, witty, attractive, single female, 35, Caribbean origin, single parent, looking for caring, down-to-earth, straight females and males for honest and genuine friendship.' So read an advertisement on the 'Lonely Hearts' page of the *Voice* newspaper. For some 'lonely hearts', life ends in fulfilment – for others, it ends in tragedy.

The *Miami Herald* tells the story of Judith Bucknell, based on her diaries. An attractive 38-year-old secretary, she had many acquaintances, but few friends. She had many lovers (fifty-nine in fifty-six months), but little love.

'Where are the men with the flowers and champagne and music?' she asked. 'Where are the men who call and ask for a genuine, actual date? Where are the men who would like to share more than my food and my bed? These are the men I would like to have in my life. Once, before I pass through my life, I should like to have the kind of sexual relationship which is part of a loving relationship.'

That day never came for Judy. She was found murdered, stabbed seven times and strangled.

Judy's final words in her diary were, 'I am alone and I want to share something with somebody.' The *Miami Herald* ended with these words: 'Judith Bucknell has failed to connect; age 38, many lovers, much love offered, none returned.'

## Does Jesus care?

One day Jesus cried, ' "My God, my God, why have you forsaken me?" ' Jesus understands the feeling of being alone. There's an old Negro spiritual which says, 'Nobody knows the trouble I've seen.' But I'm so glad that the song doesn't end there. The song concludes, 'Nobody knows, like Jesus. Glory, hallelujah!'

## Why is there so much loneliness today?

* **Firstly**, *there is an absence of the extended family.* The whole financial and emotional support system of the last millennium has just about gone. It seems that we have to pull ourselves up by our own bootstraps now.
* **Secondly**, *there is an absence of stable neighbours.* In the face of contemporary mobility, people don't stay still. It's hard to commit because there's no guarantee they'll be around tomorrow.
* **Thirdly**, *there is a lack of steady friends.* Good friends seem to be in such short supply. That's why we end up wanting that one-and-only person. Pop singer Mel C echoed the feelings of many when she said, 'I often think about what it would be like to have someone you could share everything with.'

## Does Jesus Care?

Does Jesus care when my heart
  is pained
Too deeply for mirth and song;
As the burdens press, and the
  cares distress,
And the way grows weary and long?

Oh yes, He cares – I know He cares!
His heart is touched with my grief;
When the days are weary, the long
  nights dreary,
I know my Saviour cares.

**Frank E. Graeff**

## From yuppies to dinks

First we talked about the *yuppie* – young upwardly-mobile professional person in employment. Then we had the *buppie* – Black upwardly-mobile professional person in employment. From there we had *dink* – double income no kids. And then *dinky* – double income no kids *yet*.

After that came *oink* – one income no kids. Then *lips* – low income parents supporting. And the latest sociological neologism is – ready for it? *Sinbad*. It stands for single income no boyfriend absolutely desperate! Sociologists have stated that this will be an increasingly major group as the twenty-first century progresses. But then there are the *caspars*.

In Britain, the Joseph Roundtree Foundation publishes research into demographic changes. They have witnessed the rise in single people living alone. It has put its money where its mouth is. The Foundation has invested in what they call *caspars*, an acronym for city-centre apartments for single people at affordable rents.

Who's looking out for the teenagers? More and more children are being left to their own devices after school.

## Home alone

By 2016, 4.4 million new homes will be built in Britain, despite the fact that population growth is almost static. Three groups are comprising the new demand for single households: **1)** younger people postponing marriage; **2)** the divorced and separated; and **3)** older people living together. There is a tremendous move taking place away from the traditional leave-home-get-married-set-up-new-home.

In 1971, 18% of the population were living alone. By 2016, the figure will be 36%. Statistics Canada figures show that there were 7.1 million single adults in 1999, an 18.8 per cent increase over 1990. During this period, the overall population grew by 10.1 per cent. Experts say the growth in people living alone is likely to continue. There are three reasons for this: **1)** More people are reaching old age than ever before; **2)** people are marrying later and, **3)** because of greater mobility and more disposable income, more younger persons are leaving their family home and living home alone. Meanwhile, who's looking out for the teenagers?

## Latchkey

Teenagers go to school and they are lonely. One singer said, 'I'm so lonesome I could cry.' Teenagers *do* cry; some die; some even kill. Lonely at school and lonely when they come home from school. Parents who allow their children to remain unattended or unsupervised after school and who allow their adolescents to hang out with their peers are contributing to the potential for problems. Most adolescent girls who become pregnant do so between the hours of 3 and 6pm *in their own home*.

### Latchkey kids

* In the USA 22 million adolescents are left unsupervised during the hours of 3-6pm.
* Many of these unsupervised young people spend this time with their peers.
* Adolescents are far more susceptible to peer pressure to enter into risk-taking behaviour during the unsuper vised hours between 3 and 6pm than at any other time during the day.

## It takes a village

God said, ' "It isn't good for man to be alone" ' (Genesis 2:18). We cannot fulfil our destiny alone. We all need people to help us along the way. The Africans have a proverb, 'It takes a village to raise a child.' What does this mean? Dr James Doggette, in his presentation *The Missing Link*, says if we want to know what is going on in the African culture, do not presume to understand it yourself, ask an African.

Dr Caleb Adeogun from West Africa comments in the book *Uphold That Which Is Good* that the family in Africa is largely defined by the kinship relationship within the tribe. Ministry for African families must be built upon an awareness of deeply-rooted extended family customs. Some of these, to be sure, may run counter to Christian values, but many others bring a blessing to family members and may be accommodated within a Christian understanding of family.

Dr Naphtal Rucibwa, professor of public health in Rwanda, states that marriage is not an affair of two individuals, but the affair of families. Thus divorce, while being a problem of the couple, is largely a problem of families, consequently families attempt to resolve the conflict. 'It takes a village to raise a child' simply means that you are not alone, everybody gets in on the act! That village may be defined by geographical borders, but the mentality extends beyond. The reality of the extended family is felt by people of African descent everywhere.

Dr Charles Bradford says, 'There is a spiritual connection, a visceral unity, between and among the African peoples that is unique. Like separated twins who somehow mysteriously share the same feelings across the years, though miles apart, Africans on the continent and Africans in diaspora exhibit a symbiotic connection that W. E. B. DuBois often referred to as "the blood" ' (*Sabbath Roots: The Africa Connection*).

Alex Haley, the author of *Roots*, had in his office a picture of a turtle sitting atop a fencepost. Under it, the caption read, 'You can be sure he didn't get up there by himself.' We need to realize that we are part of a great network of humanity and we all need each other. At the same time, we are individuals and we are unique.

## No one like me

Og Mandino said, 'Since the beginning of time never has there been another with my mind, my heart, my eyes, my ears, my hands, my hair, my mouth. None that came before, none that lives today, and none that comes tomorrow can walk and talk and move and think exactly like me. All men are my brothers yet I am different from each. I am a unique creature. No one can duplicate my brushstrokes, none can

## We all need each other

There is a wonderful fable that tells of a young girl who is walking through a meadow when she sees a butterfly impaled upon a thorn. Very carefully she releases it and the butterfly starts to fly away. Then it comes back and changes into a beautiful good fairy. 'For your kindness,' she tells the little girl, 'I will grant you your fondest wish.' The little girl thinks for a moment and replies, 'I want to be happy.' The fairy leans towards her and whispers in her ear and then suddenly vanishes.

As the girl grew, no one in the land was more happy than she. Whenever anyone asked her for the secret of her happiness, she would only smile and say, 'I listened to a good fairy.' As she grew quite old, the neighbours were afraid the fabulous secret might die with her. 'Tell us, please,' they begged, 'tell us what the fairy said.' The now lovely old lady simply smiled and said, 'She told me that everyone, no matter how secure they seemed, had need of me!' We all need each other.

**Leo Buscaglia,** *Loving Each Other: The Challenge of Human Relationships*

make my chisel marks, none can duplicate my handwriting, and none can produce my child. I am different from all others, and proud of the difference. I am a unique creature of nature. I am rare, and there is value in all rarity; therefore I am valuable.'

Don't try to fill anyone else's shoes. With God and the Bible as your standard, put your own spin on life. We need it! We need you! The world needs *your* brand of love, *your* sort of personality, *your* type of humour. The world needs to see life wearing *your* clothes, seen through *your* lenses. It's *your* web page we need to see. We need your smile, your warmth. We may not always have told you that we appreciate you – but we're telling you now! We love you and we need you! Don't deprive us! Don't give up on us! Don't give up on life!

## *Alone – Really?*

***I am alone***

*I don't have a partner like so many of my friends*
*I don't have as good a personality as that guy*
*I am not as good looking as that girl*
*I used to be married; I've never been married*
*I'm a woman, I'm black, I'm Hispanic*
*I'm physically-challenged*
*What have I got to give?*
*I've got so much to give*
*I am already giving so much*
*I'm different, but I'm special*
*I love me for who I am*
*I have family members who love me*
*I have people who like my company*
*I can develop friendships with older people, younger people*

***I am not really alone***

## Getting beyond the myths of singleness

**Myth 1:** *Singles are immature.* We tend to see marriage and children as the true benchmarks of maturity. Regardless of actual age, single women may be referred to as 'girls'. Single men may be dismissed as fun-loving or too self-centred to get on with life.

**Myth 2:** *Singles are incomplete.* Because humans are social beings who seek relationships, love and a way to express their sexuality, we think married people are normal and single people are, perhaps, uh . . . abnormal.

**Myth 3:** *Singles are unstable.* Because the myth of restlessness persists, it is difficult for many singles to get jobs, obtain credit, buy a home, be taken seriously in their careers, earn equal pay, be considered for promotions, or adopt children.

**Myth 4:** *Singles are damaged.* If people never marry, we wonder what is wrong with them. If they divorce or separate, we wonder what is wrong with them. If their partner dies and they don't remarry, we wonder what is wrong with them.

**Myth 5:** *Singles are dangerous.* Few couples are 100 per cent secure in their marriage. When singles arrive, married people's internal radar systems may start flashing. They may wonder: Is this innocent friendship or subtle flirtation? Is it safe to socialize? What if singles are homosexual – should we hold them at arm's length and deny them contact with children?

**Myth 6:** *Singles are inconsequential.* Some people think numbers are truth. With numbers they define who is important and who is not. Fifty-one per cent may matter, but five per cent probably doesn't. Singles are marginal in society's 'big picture'.

**Myth 7:** *Singles are unacceptable.* For all these reasons singles may feel unacceptable. An exception is made if you are single and under 25: young singles may feel anxious, but they are OK if their singleness is clearly temporary.

**Kit Watts** (adapted)

Paula Webber says in the book, *Profiles of Service,* 'With God on my side, I don't believe in giving up until the task is done.' You need others and others need you. As the mouse said to the elephant as they walked across the bridge, 'My, didn't *we* shake that bridge!'

## Sometimes I don't like myself

Candace Sharp tells of how her younger sister Melody received all the attention at home – until seven years later. That was when their mother brought home a new baby and, over the next few years, added two more. Melody was devastated. Without warning, she was shoved out of her birth-order niche. She rapidly put on weight, became the rebel of the family, struggled with low self-esteem and had a disastrous first marriage. It wasn't until she was secure in her value to God that she was able to deal with the weight problem and had a strong second marriage.

At the age of 39, Melody was struck with a sudden brain haemorrhage. She died three days later. At the funeral, Candace was overwhelmed with the number of friends who came to tell her how Melody had positively affected their lives. Apparently, she had a giving nature, and everybody knew they could count on her to drop everything to lend a hand if they needed it.

When the funeral ended, several family members went over to the coffin to say their final goodbyes. It was then that Candace discovered that the not-good-enoughs had continued to plague Melody all her life.

In her book, *Sometimes I Don't Like Myself,* Candace Sharp writes the following: 'Her husband's softly spoken words stunned me: "Oh, Melody," he said, "you would have loved this. You never thought that people really liked you." '

'Yet,' says Candace, 'she had overcome. She had lived a happy life because she had identified the things that made her insecure. She had named her enemies and did not let them have the victory over her but told them No. Most of all, she knew the deep and abiding love of God.'

Not pretty enough. Not skinny enough. Not outgoing enough. It's one thing to struggle – it's another thing when you have to struggle alone. Somebody said most people lead lives of quiet desperation. This can certainly be true for the next group.

## Homosexuality

If there is any group of single people who feel alone, it is homosexuals. Many today are finding out that some of their closest friends and relatives are homosexuals. When homosexuals decide to become Christians, the church asks should homosexuals **1)** change their orientation; **2)** control their orientation; or **3)** celebrate their orientation?

Some say that homosexuality is as a result of choice or a consequence of a chain of circumstances resulting in being marginalized by society (known as *situational).* Others simply say they were born that way (known as *constitutional).* Dr Samuel Koranteng-Pipim, in his paper *Born A Gay or Born Again,* says we are faced with three options: **1)** non acceptance; **2)** partial acceptance; or **3)** full acceptance.

## Non-acceptance

Those who hold to the *non-acceptance* position believe that homosexuality is a post-fall *distortion* or a deviation from God's plan for human sexuality. Homosexuals can *change* by the power of God. They believe that the Church should welcome those who acknowledge the sinfulness of homosexuality, accept Christ's offer of forgiveness, and commit themselves to a life of sexual purity.

## Partial acceptance

Those who hold to the *partial acceptance* position believe that homosexuality is a post-fall *aberration* or deviation from God's plan for human sexuality. They believe that homosexuals must *control* their homosexual drives through self-discipline and the power of God. Those who remain homosexual celibates should be fully welcomed into the Church family.

## Full acceptance

Those who hold to the *full acceptance* position believe that homosexuality is the post-fall *natural order*, or God's design. They are to *celebrate* God's gift and should not only be part of the Church, but should be allowed to date, marry and have children.

## What can we do?

Christianity does not condone the practice of homosexuality. One Church's affirmation of marriage and sexual behaviour declares:

'Marriage was divinely established in Eden and affirmed by Jesus Christ to be both monogamous and heterosexual, a lifelong union of loving companionship between a man and a woman. Sexual practices which are contrary to God's expressed will are adultery and premarital sex, as well as obsessive sexual behaviour. Sexual abuse of spouses, sexual abuse of children, incest, *homosexual practices (gay and lesbian)*, and bestiality are among the obvious perversions of God's original plan.'

## 1 Corinthians 6:9-11 reads:

'Do you not know that the unrighteous will not inherit the kingdom of God? Do not be deceived. Neither fornicators, nor idolaters, nor adulterers, nor homosexuals, nor sodomites, nor thieves, nor covetous, nor drunkards, nor revilers, nor extortioners will inherit the kingdom of God. *And such were some of you. But you were washed, but you were sanctified, but you were justified in the name of the Lord Jesus and by the Spirit of our God.'* (Italics supplied, NKJV)

The passage teaches us the following:
**1)** it suggests that homosexuality is no worse than other sins;
**2)** it provides hope for change to the homosexual; the phrase 'such were some of you' places all these sinful lifestyles in the past tense;
**3)** it reveals sources of help; 'in the name of the Lord Jesus and by the Spirit of our God'.

While homosexual practice *is* a sin, homosexual practice is not the only sin or

## Spiritual Incurables?

They repeatedly asked me, 'Why can't the church help us, too? The church has marriage seminars, social action ministries for the poor, prayer for the sick – why can't they help us, too?

'Why must we be singled out as spiritual incurables? Why must we continue to be outcasts? Why can't the church move beyond rejection and see us as hurting people who want help just like other sinners?'

I was forced to admit that I really didn't know; maybe it was because of pastors like me who need to learn that hating sin meant something other than hating sinners.

I needed to experience that move from revulsion to compassion that allowed me to reject the sin without rejecting the sinner – to accept the person without embracing his/her problem. I needed to be reminded and then to remind others that Jesus died for *homosexuals*, was raised from the dead for *homosexuals*, and that His power was available to deliver all sinners from their sins.

Even homosexuals.

Don Baker

the worst sin. There is healing and forgiveness available from God and there must be compassion from church members. It is important, *for the spiritual growth of the church members,* that they extend compassion instead of homophobia at best and condemnation at worst.

Many homosexuals are closet homosexuals. They are afraid to request prayer at church for fear of encouraging the wrath and rejection of the very people who understand they are to 'bear one another's burdens and thus fulfil the law of Christ' (Galatians 6:2).

We must always display the welcome mat of acceptance. Homosexuals, bisexuals, transvestites, all must see the Church saying to them, This is the place for you. The Church's secret agenda is that the spirit of God is powerful enough to work a change. We believe that.

There are organizations committed to helping individuals in that struggle. Martin Hallett, author of *Out of the Blue: Responding Compassionately to Homosexuality,* is Director of True Freedom Trust, a Christian organization helping people with homosexual feelings, their relatives and friends, to talk about and cope with their sexual orientation. Our job is not to condemn them for God, it is to commit them to God, if you like, *to struggle together.* For no matter if we've been Christians for five or fifty years, each of us is wearing a sign saying, 'Please be patient with me, God is not through with me yet.'

## Sick and tired?

Can loneliness lead to sickness? Well, there are three ailments we need to stay clear of:

* **Somebody sickness.** This is the belief that there is one person out there who can make you happy. Merle Shain says, 'There is no perfect person who can make you whole. The only way you ever feel strong and sure is when you are giving to others instead of wishing that they would give to you.'
* **Yesterday blues.** That's when you look at the past, the so-called good old days. After all, didn't everybody find a partner in those days? *No they didn't!* Shake yourself from your dream-world fantasy and face today's reality. Don't get stuck in yesterday. Paul said, 'I am still not all I should be but I am bringing all my energies to

## Singles' Prayer

Dear Heavenly Father:

Our confidence in You is strong and firm. We are thankful that our situation is no mystery to You. Calm our spirits with that thought. Show us how we can not only accept our single state, but flourish in it. There are unique difficulties we live with – misunderstanding, times of intense loneliness, distinct feelings of rejection, and very real temptations most people can't possibly imagine.

But we are confident You will use even these troubles to mature our walk. We do so desire to glorify Your name and to minister to others in an authentic and meaningful manner. Encourage us by opening doors of opportunity, then make us sensitive to You and bold in faith as we step through those doors to serve others who need what we can provide.

In the strong name of Christ. Amen.

Charles Swindoll, *Singleness*

'Today should be savoured, not gulped down. If you don't learn how to stop and enjoy today, you'll never enjoy one day of the future either.'

bear on this one thing: forgetting the past and looking forward to what lies ahead, I strain to reach the end of the race' (Philippians 3:13).

* **Destination disease.** That's when you think, if only I could get to that place or achieve that goal. Recognize that your happiest moments are not at the end of the trip but *along the way!* Dr Mike Murdock says in his book, *Secrets of the Journey,* 'Today should be savoured, not gulped down. If you don't learn how to stop and enjoy today, you'll never enjoy one day of the future either.'

## One day at a time

A popular Country and Western song says, 'One day at a time, sweet Jesus, that's all I'm asking from You . . . .' And in the final analysis, though our loneliness is often unbearable, we can only take life one day at a time. This was never more clearly illustrated to me than when I was living in West Africa.

I was in a village of the Ashanti tribe of Ghana waiting for a bus. The group around me were sitting happily. After a while I said to them, 'Excuse me, what time is the bus coming?' They said, 'Don't worry, soon come.' I waited, looked at my watch, then repeated my question. They repeated their answer. After a while, it started to get dark. 'I'm sorry to disturb you,' I said, 'but is the bus really coming?' 'Oh, don't worry,' they said, 'if it doesn't come today it will come tomorrow.'

I thought about Matthew 6:34, ' "So don't be anxious about tomorrow. God will take care of your tomorrow too. Live one day at a time." '

# Solowork on Chapter 2

## What's important to me?

Singleness is a time to clarify values, to make yourself aware of what means the most to you. Dr Elsie Jackson shared with me the following exercise:

You are going on a very long voyage across the ocean to a new land. The land is largely agricultural. It has been strongly influenced by former British rulers, and it is formal in its dress and customs. The climate is tropical all year round. Most people live and work on the farms, but the ruling class live luxuriously and the hotels have first-class facilities. The countryside is beautiful, with many mountains and lakes. You can take *only one suitcase which will hold about 7 items.* Anything you cannot put in the suitcase will have to be left behind. Make a list of what you will take and then discuss it with your friends! NB You cannot buy anything while you are there and you will be gone for 15-20 years.

1) ______________________

2) ______________________

3) ______________________

4) ______________________

5) ______________________

6) ______________________

7) ______________________

## READ ON!

| Author | Book title | Publisher |
| --- | --- | --- |
| Baker, Don | Beyond Rejection: The Church, Homosexuality and Hope | Multnomah Books |
| Edwards, Haskell G. | The Imigrant Family: Framework for Adaptation and Excellence | Maracle Press |
| Matteson, Richard & Harris, Janis Long | What if I married the wrong person? | Bethany House |

# Chapter 3

# Could it be I'm falling in love?

Dear Dr Brown

How can one determine God's leading when it comes to courtship?

I have never dated around in church. I have always maintained that I do not want to be Tom, Dick and Harry's ex-girlfriend. The idea that a number of men can say, 'I know what it's like to be with Mary' has never appealed to me. I don't want to date around now. I would like very much for God to provide me with a companion. I have asked God to take control of every aspect of my life because He has foresight and never makes a mistake. I cannot see a man's heart or mind but God can, which is why I prefer to trust His leading. My problem is, I'm not always able to work out His leading, and I find this extremely frustrating.

There's a young man in a nearby city to whom I'm attracted. I believe he is aware because, against my wishes, a so-called friend felt the need to tell him. She also felt the need to flirt with him and attract his attention. Then she had the audacity to let me know how close they had become within a few weeks, basically telling me to back off.

I was disappointed but wondered whether this was God intervening. I'm not certain and I wish I could be. Despite this young lady wanting to give me the impression that they were courting, I have discovered from other sources that they're not.

Last weekend I saw him at a concert quite by chance. He was as handsome as ever. I told him about a 'dinner-do' I was having for my birthday and invited him. He was very non-committal and basically said if he wasn't busy he'd consider it. I found this offensive, but didn't let it show.

I wish I could forget about him completely or stop viewing him as a prospective partner. Sometimes when someone is attracted to you, you can feel it. I felt none of this with him.

I do accept that God may have something better lined up for me (Jeremiah 29:11). Also, I do not believe two people coming together should be so much hard work, though I am a firm believer in working hard for whatever I believe is valuable, like my education for instance. I do not know whether I can apply this to engaging the interest of this young man.

He is a very marketable young man and he is aware of this. He is also aware that a lot of girls would like to be his partner, but I would like to get to know him, an opportunity which seems to elude me. But most importantly, how can I decipher God's leading?

Mary

The dating game. It is just that. A game.

## Dating – it's a set-up!

Joshua Harris, in his book *I Kissed Dating Goodbye,* tells of how he was at the altar with his bride, about to get married, when a young lady came up, took his other arm, and stood at his side. Before he could ask her what she was doing, another young lady joined her, then another, then another, until finally there were six of them by his side.

'What are you doing here?' Joshua asked. 'I'm here to get married,' one said. 'And me, and me!' chimed the others. 'You gave me a piece of your heart, remember?' said one. 'You said you'd never met anyone like me before,' said another. 'You said I was the only one for you,' said still another. 'That's what he said to me!' chorused the others. Joshua's bride looked at him in shock. 'You didn't tell me all of this!' she cried. 'Oh, but sweetheart,' he said, 'Everything that's left is yours!' His bride fled the scene in a flood of tears. It was then that Joshua – woke up.

Yes, just a dream, but not fiction. You hear the expression all the time – *the dating game*. And it is just that. A game – a game of hit and miss, luck and chance, try-it-out-for-size, use-it-and-throw-it-away. Dr Hyveth Williams said at a singles seminar in London, 'Dating is the biggest set-up for failure in a relationship because we behave our best to impress and when we have caught the fish we want, we see him or her for who they really are!'

Almost every book we read on the subject wants to give us guidelines as to how to play the game to win, but who said we need to play the game at all? Only in a minority of societies is dating actually practised, it's just that these are the societies that publish the most books! So it looks like everybody's doing it, but they're not.

Here's a book I recommend – the book of Romans! In chapter 12 and verse 2 the apostle Paul counsels us: 'Don't copy the behaviour and customs of this world, but be a new and different person with a fresh newness in all you do and think. Then you will learn from your own experience how his ways will really satisfy you.'

## Two by two?

In societies where dating is *not* practised – *the majority of societies* – young people listen to the advice of their elders regarding the choice of a mate. Young people can go out in groups – they do not have to pair off in twos like animals entering Noah's ark. They do not have to try Mary out and try Peter out in an intimate just-the-two-of-us situation.

Marriage experts David and Vera Mace believe that the intense feelings of youth should be balanced with the detached judgement of more mature experience, thus, they say, 'the desirable ideal, we believe, is a co-operative selection by young people and parents together.'

# A Date With Fate

Jenny was so happy about the house they had found.
For once in her life 'twas on the right side of town.
She unpacked her things with such great ease.
As she watched her new curtains blow in the breeze.

How wonderful it was to have her own room.
School would be starting, she'd have friends over soon.
There'd be sleep-overs, and parties; she was so happy
It's just the way she wanted her life to be.

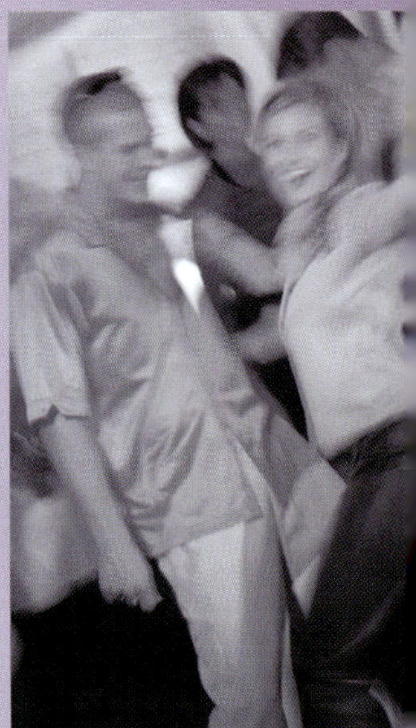

On the first day of school, everything went great.
She made new friends and even got a date!
She thought, 'I want to be popular and I'm going to be,
Because I just got a date with the star of the team!'

To be known in this school you had to have clout,
And dating this guy would sure help her out.
There was only one problem stopping her fate:
Her parents had said she was too young to date.

'Well I just won't tell them the entire truth.
They won't know the difference; what's there to lose?'
Jenny asked to stay with her friends that night.
Her parents frowned but said, 'All right.'

Excited, she got ready for the big event.
But as she rushed around like she had no sense,
She began to feel guilty about all the lies,
But what's a pizza, a party, and a moonlight ride?

Well, the pizza was good, and the party was great,
But the moonlight ride would have to wait.
For Jeff was half drunk by this time.
But he kissed her and said that he was just fine.

Then the room filled with smoke and Jeff took a puff.
Jenny couldn't believe he was smoking that stuff.
Now Jeff was ready to ride to the point
But only after he'd smoked the rest of the joint.

They jumped in the car for the moonlight ride,
Not thinking that he was too drunk to drive.
They finally made it to the point at last,
And Jeff started trying to make a pass.

A pass is not what Jenny wanted at all
(and by a pass, I don't mean playing football.)
'Perhaps my parents were right. . . . maybe I am too young.
Boy, how could I ever, ever be so dumb?'

With all of her might, she pushed Jeff away:
'Please take me home, I don't want to stay.'
Jeff cranked up the engine and floored the gas.
In a matter of seconds they were going too fast.

As Jeff drove on in a fit of wild anger,
Jenny knew that her life was in danger.
She begged and pleaded for him to slow down,
But he just got faster as they neared the town.

'Just let me get home! I'll confess that I lied.
I really went out for a moonlight ride.'
Then all of a sudden, she saw a big flash.
'Oh, God, please help us! We're going to crash!'

She doesn't remember the force of impact.
Just that everything all of a sudden went black.
She felt someone remove her from the twisted rubble,
And heard, 'Call an ambulance! These kids are in trouble!'

Voices she heard . . . a few words at best.
But she knew there were two cars involved in the wreck.
Then wondered to herself if Jeff was all right,
And if the people in the other car were alive.

She awoke in the hospital to faces so sad.
'You've been in a wreck and it looks pretty bad.'
These voices echoed inside her head,
As they gently told her that Jeff was dead.

They said, 'Jenny, we've done all we can do.
But it looks as if we'll lose you too.'
'But the people in the other car?' Jenny cried.
'We're sorry, Jenny, they also died.'

Jenny prayed, 'God, forgive me for what I've done;
I only wanted to have just one night of fun.'
'Tell those people's family, I've made their lives dim,
And wish I could return their families to them.'

'Tell Mum and Dad I'm sorry I lied,
And that it's my fault so many have died.
This great tragedy really didn't have to be,
Oh, nurse, won't you please tell them that for me?'

The nurse just stood there – she never agreed
To pass on the words of her patient in need.
She took Jenny's hand with tears in her eyes.
And a few moments later Jenny died.

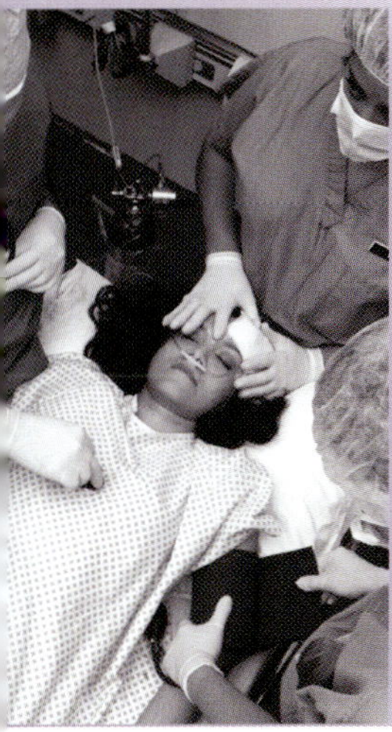

A man asked the nurse, 'Why didn't you do your best
To bid that girl her one last request?'
She looked at the man with eyes so sad.
'Because the people in the other car were her mum and dad.'

This story is sad and unpleasant but true,
So people take heed – it could have been you.

Anonymous

## *Falling* in love?

You see her with a black eye. 'How did you get that? And don't tell me you walked into a door. It was your boyfriend Tom, wasn't it? Why don't you just leave him? He's no good for you.' That's when you hear the familiar response. 'Oh, I know he drinks, I know he smokes, and I know he knocks me around sometimes, but I can't help myself, I just love him.' Is that love or is it infatuation? Halsey Peat, an expert on premarital counselling says, 'Love is not stupid. Common sense must not be ignored. Recognize when you are being used and if you cannot change it, get away from it.'

Some people call it falling in love. Psychologist Eric Fromm tells us that love is 'an activity, not a passive affect; it is a "standing in", not a "falling for".' But love is not a hole that you can't help stepping into. As Dr Errol Lawrence from Canadian University College says in his paper *The Spirituality of Marriage,* 'People do not fall in love. They grow in love. Usually, anything so delicate as love will break if it falls.'

# Love versus Infatuation

| Love: | Infatuation: |
|---|---|
| is patient and allows time for the relationship to grow. | is impatient, rash, impulsive, and unreasonable. |
| is self-controlled and wants the best for the other and the relationship. | is self-willed and demands its own way. |
| looks beyond the external and is attracted also by the character traits. It is person centred. | is preoccupied by external qualities which arouse passion and lust. It is sex-centred. |
| cannot be separated from the One who *is* love. Love and faith therefore go together, love giving meaning to faith and faith giving purpose to love. | is caught up with present sensations and often leads individuals away from God. |
| is built on self-acceptance and assumes the best in the other by implicit trust. | is often unsure of self and therefore jealous and possessive of the other; shows itself by constant quarrelling. |
| is built on friendship and leaves individuals better for having known each other *even if they break up.* | has an unsure basis and leaves behind scars and painful memories should the couple break up. |
| is truthful and is characterized by open and honest communication. | plays games because of the fear of sharing the real self and being rejected. |
| is true to personal values even if it may risk loss of the relationship. | may cause individuals to do what is wrong for fear of losing each other. |
| weathers the ups and downs of life with the realization that feelings and circumstances do not alter the commitment to be loving. | is moody and creates a certain nervousness about the relationship. |
| makes one a better person. | has traumas which drain a person of energy so school, work and home relationships suffer. One becomes irritable and 'different'. |
| adds to self-confidence. | tends to breed dependency and a poor feeling about oneself. |
| grows with time and lasts despite separation. | weakens with time and separation. |

I say if you're going to go into a hole, choose a good one! Have some criteria so that you'll listen to what your head says instead of how your heart sways. Ask yourself, is he respectful of his elders? Does he want to better himself and you? How does he treat his mother and sister/s? Is he respectful of me? Does he love children? Does he love God?

## Family of origin

We are all caught up in looking high and low for a good partner. Well, he or she may be nearer than you think – may even be in your own church! We admire Hollywood figures whom we know nothing about, but we see them commit early and after 90 minutes of screen-time, the two go off into the sunset, having had no previous knowledge of one another, supposedly to live happily ever after.

There are patterns of family background that you would do well to pay attention to; patterns of divorce, adultery and abuse. In fact, family patterns, while being by no means infallible, are the best predictor of marital happiness. Look before you leap.

## Love – art or science?

One of America's well-known senators, William Proxmire, made national headlines when he severely criticized the National Science Foundation for 'squandering' federal funds. Why? Because it had made a grant aimed at serious study of 'romantic love'.

Hollywood sunset romances are not necessarily the norm.

'I object to this,' said Proxmire. 'I'm against it because I don't want the answer. I believe that 200 million other Americans want to leave some things in life a mystery. And right at the top of things we don't want to know is why a man falls in love with a woman and vice versa. No, National Science Foundation – get out of the love racket. Here, if anywhere, Alexander Pope was right when he observed, "If ignorance is bliss, 'tis folly to be wise." '

## Topics covered in Premarital Counselling

- Temperament
- Spirituality
- Family background
- Communication
- Conflict resolution
- Role expectations
- Sexual understanding
- Finance
- Leisure
- Wedding
- Children
- Mission of the home

## Intelligence or intuition?

This attitude reminds me of the news reporter who objected to taking a premarital counselling inventory because she preferred some things about her future partner to remain a mystery. Why do we demand intelligence for everything else, but intuition for marriage? Make no mistake about it, love *is* a mystery! Solomon declared, 'There are three things too wonderful for me to understand – no, four! How an eagle glides through the sky. How a serpent crawls upon a rock. How a ship finds its way across the heaving ocean. The growth of love between a man and a girl.' Proverbs 30:18, 19. But surely something so wonderful as love should make us careful to get the most out of it.

Abraham Maslow declared, 'Our duty is clear. We must understand love. We must be able to teach it, to create it, to predict it, or else the world is lost to hostility and to suspicion.'

## Maximum rewards, minimum expense

So people are now making intense studies on love and why we like some people more than others. Research has shown that we are attracted to people who bring us *maximum rewards or gratification at minimum expense.*

We like people who satisfy our needs and who have needs we can satisfy.

What does that mean?

Well, we are more attracted to people who are nearby than to people who are far away. We like people who are already attracted to us, and who demonstrate their attraction by doing us favours and saying nice things about us. We like people who satisfy our needs and who have needs we can satisfy.

## Love by association

Then there is the *two-component theory* of love. This states that people's emotional experience is a function of the cognitive labels they attach to their feelings of physiological arousal. In other words, *any sort of physiological arousal can be interpreted as passionate love if the conditions are right.*

Take a woman at a concert. If she is enjoying the concert and exhilarated by the music *and* sitting next to an attractive date, she is likely to transfer her emotions for the concert to her emotions for her date. In fact she is likely to interpret her arousal as romantic passion because her date is close by; she loves the music – she loves him! A woman who goes to the concert and finds her emotions are aroused by the music will interpret those emotions differently if she goes alone – or with her mother!

Beware love by association . . .

## Love by fear

There is also the *fear-reduction* model of love. This says that even negative sources of arousal can, under the right conditions, facilitate romantic passion. Take the man who has received some bad news.

Where he works is coming under new management and it's a case of last hired first fired. He's worried about losing his job. A neighbour comforts him. Next week the news comes – he's fired. He runs back to the neighbour. She comforts him again. A relationship starts to develop. You hear them say, 'I don't know how it happened, we just seem right for each other.' We know how it happened. It's called fear-reduction. *We are more attracted to people who reduce our negative arousal by allaying our fears and calming our anger.*

## Love by science

In the last few years even the scientists have got in on the love thing. They have said that when you experience love it's not just the emotions of the heart, even the chemicals in your body start to react. When you fall in love, the body is literally flooded by the chemical cousins of amphetamines: dopamine, norepinephrine and, especially, phenylethylamine. When you get to the going steady or attachment stage, larger amounts of endorphins flow into the brain. That's when you get that relaxed, calm, secure sensation that makes you say, Yes, he's going away to the University of Alaska, but I know everything's going to work out fine.

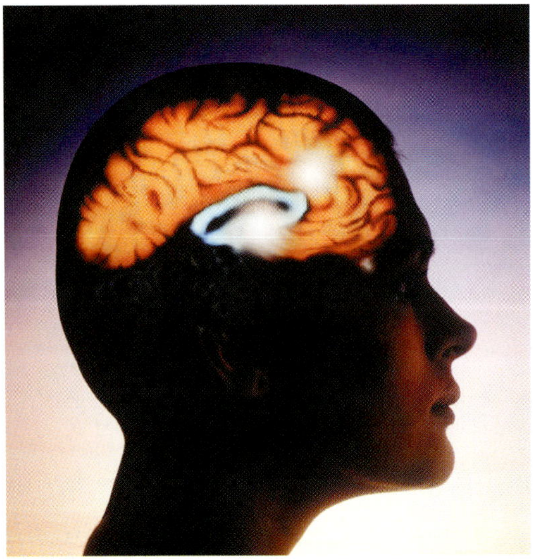

Love, an exact science? Probably not or definitely not?

## One-sided love

But I want to focus on Sternberg's theory of love. There are three aspects to complete love, like three sides of a triangle, and they give rise to eight possible love triangles:

- When none of these three components is present you have ***nonlove***. This actually represents the majority of our relationships. Just casual interactions. It's your relationship with the newsagent, the bank teller, the postman, just casual – well at least I hope so!
- The second kind of love is ***liking***. Now we have one side of the triangle filled in – ***intimacy***. This doesn't refer to anything physical, it's how well you communicate, share your inner feelings, your time, yourself. You can talk to the person, tell them all about yourself. It's what you have in a true friendship, closeness and warmth.
- The third triangle does not have intimacy but has something else – ***passion***. Love at first sight – ***infatuation***. There's a lot of physical activity, from hugging, kissing, to touching and making love. It can come quickly and it can go quickly because there's no intimacy and you do not have the third side of the triangle – ***commitment***.

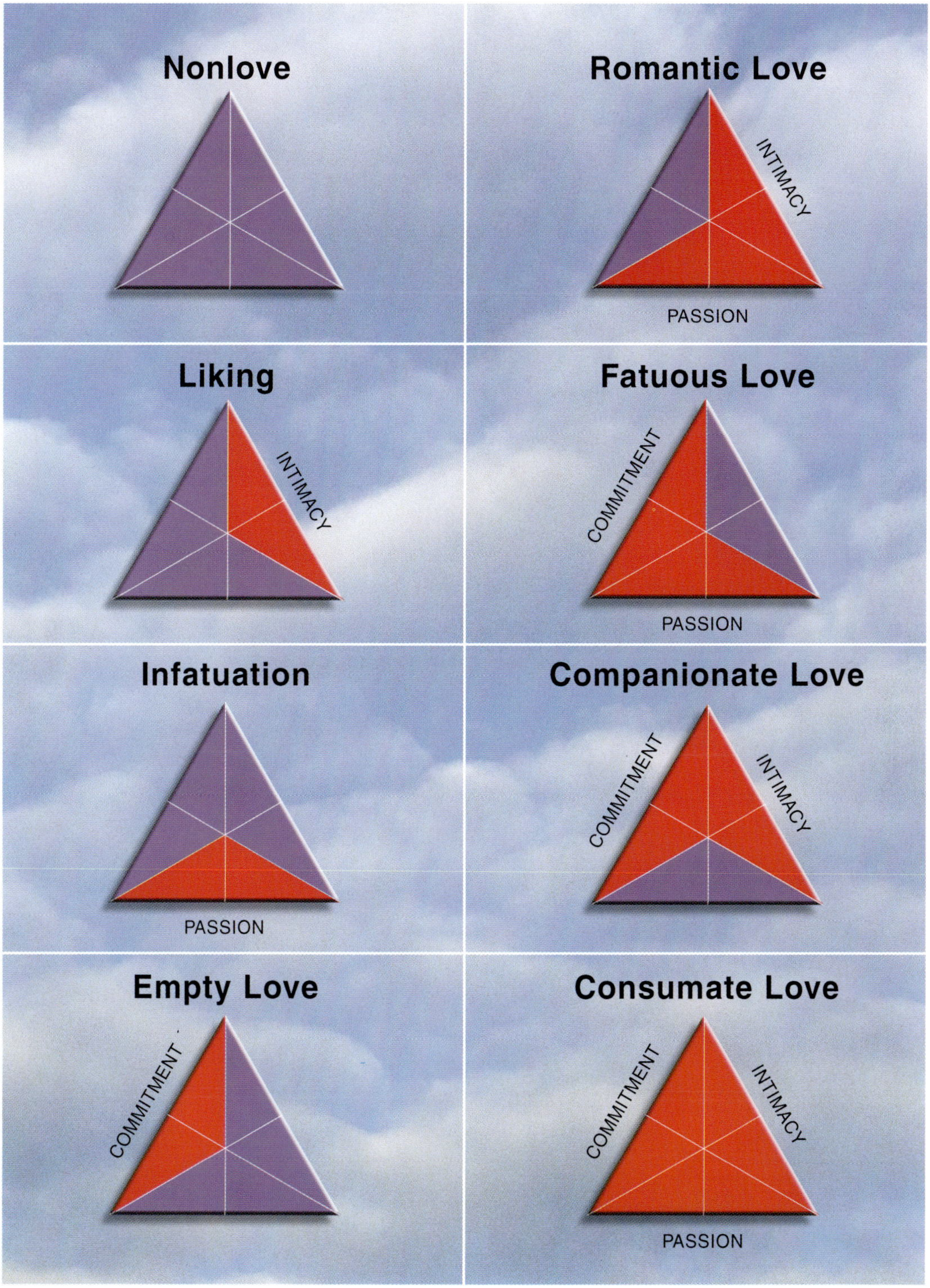
Nonlove
Romantic Love
INTIMACY
PASSION
Liking
INTIMACY
Fatuous Love
COMMITMENT
PASSION
Infatuation
PASSION
Companionate Love
COMMITMENT
INTIMACY
Empty Love
COMMITMENT
Consumate Love
COMMITMENT
INTIMACY
PASSION

❤ Commitment includes trust, staying together through the hard times, for better or for worse. But if commitment is all you have then you've got ***empty love***. You see it sometimes in a 30 year-old marriage that has become stagnant. The couple used to be intimate but they don't talk any more. They used to be passionate, but that's died out. All that's left is a grin-and-bear-it decision to stay together. Empty love.

## Two-sided love

❤ Let's see what happens when you have more than one of these components. Well, if you have intimacy and passion you've got ***romantic love***. It's more than infatuation; you talk well together. You meet on your summer holiday, at summer school or summer camp. It's romantic but it's not going to last because he's going back to Brazil or she's going home to Barcelona. It's romantic, but the best you usually

get is a promise to keep in touch.

❤ Now passion plus commitment is called ***fatuous love***. It's what you often see in Hollywood. Very physical and next month married. It's the passion which binds them together and because intimacy takes time to develop they don't have what it takes emotionally to make the relationship work.

❤ What about commitment and intimacy, but no passion? It's called ***companionate love***, a long-term friendship or the kind of marriages with committed love and intimacy but diminished physical attraction. Elaine and William Walster, in *A New Look at Love,* say this: 'By the time passion flickers out, it has been replaced by companionate love – shared understandings, emotions, and habits. Passionate love is a fragile flower; it wilts in time. Companionate love is an evergreen; it thrives with contact.'

## Getting in shape

❤ What happens when you've got all three sides of the triangle? Then you're in shape! You have what's called ***consummate love***, or complete love. When your passion is balanced by your intimacy and your intimacy is balanced by your commitment you have the kind of love towards which many people strive. It's not easy. It's like losing weight – oh, you can lose it in a week, but trying to keep the weight off, that's the hard part! Trying to keep the relationship balanced, that's the hard part. The good news is, it's difficult, but it's not impossible.

## **Appointment with love** – looking beyond the external

**Six minutes to six,** said the clock over the information booth in New York's Grand Central Station. The tall young army lieutenant lifted his sunburned face, and narrowed his eyes to note the exact time. His heart was pounding with a beat that shocked him. In six minutes he would see the woman who had filled such a special place in his life for the past thirteen months, the woman he had never seen, yet whose written words had sustained him unfailingly.

Lieutenant Blandford remembered one day in particular, the worst of the fighting, when his plane had been caught in the middle of a pack of enemy planes.

In one of his letters he had confessed to her that he often felt fear, and only a few days before this battle he had received her answer: 'Of course you fear . . . all brave men do. Next time you doubt yourself, I want you to hear my voice reciting to you: "Yea, though I walk through the valley of the shadow of death, I shall fear no evil; for Thou art with me."' He had remembered, and it had renewed his strength.

Now he was going to hear her real voice. Four minutes to six.

A girl passed close to him, and Lieutenant Blandford gave a start. She was wearing a flower, but it was not the little red rose they had agreed upon. Besides, this girl was only about 18, and Hollis Meynell had told him she was 30. 'What of it?' he had answered. 'I'm 32.' He was 29.

His mind went back to that book he had read in the training camp. *Of Human Bondage,* it was called; and throughout the book were notes in a woman's handwriting. He had never believed that a woman could see into a man's heart so tenderly, so understandingly. Her name was on the bookplate: Hollis Meynell. He had obtained a New York telephone book and found her address. He had written, she had answered. Next day he had been shipped out, but they had gone on writing.

For thirteen months she had faithfully replied. When his letters did not arrive, she wrote anyway, and now he believed he loved her, and she loved him.

But she had refused all his pleas to send him her photograph. She had explained: If your feeling for me has any reality, what I look like won't matter. Suppose I'm beautiful. I'd always be haunted by the feeling that you had been taking a chance on just that, and that kind of love would disturb me. Suppose I'm plain (and you must admit that this is more likely), then I'd always fear that you were only going on writing because you were lonely and had no one else. No, don't ask for my picture. When you come to New York, you shall see me and then you shall make your decision.'

One minute to six . . . Lieutenant Blandford's heart leaped.

A young woman was coming towards him. Her figure was long and slim; her blonde hair lay back in curls from her delicate ears. Her eyes were blue as flowers, her lips and chin had a gentle firmness. In her pale-green suit she was like springtime come alive.

He started toward her, forgetting to notice that she was wearing no rose. As he moved, a small, provocative smile curved her lips.

'Going my way, soldier?' she murmured.

He made one step closer to her. Then he saw Hollis Meynell.

She was standing almost directly behind the girl, a woman well past 40, her greying hair tucked under a worn hat. She was more than plump; her thick-ankled feet were thrust into low-heeled shoes. But she wore a red rose on her rumpled coat. The girl in the green suit was walking quickly away.

Blandford felt as though he were being split in two, so keen was his desire to follow the girl, yet so deep was his longing for the woman whose spirit had truly companioned and upheld his own; and there she stood. He could see that her pale, plump face was gentle and sensible; her grey eyes had a warm twinkle.

Lieutenant Blandford did not hesitate. His fingers gripped the worn copy of *Of Human Bondage* which was to identify him to her. This would not be love, but it would be something precious, a friendship for which he had been and must ever be grateful . . . .

He squared his shoulders, saluted, and held the book out towards the woman, although even while he spoke he felt the bitterness of his disappointment.

'I'm Lieutenant John Blandford, and you – you are Miss Meynell. I'm so glad you could meet me. May – may I take you to dinner?' The woman's face broadened into a tolerant smile.

'I don't know what this is all about, son,' she answered. 'That young lady in the green suit, she begged me to wear this rose on my coat. And she said that if you asked me to go out with you, I should tell you she's waiting for you in that restaurant across the street. She said it was some kind of a test.'

Anonymous

## Control the Computer

I'm not referring to the electronic encyclopaedia, I'm talking about those dating chat rooms. You will end up in an old-fashioned word – sin. Sin will take you further than you planned to go; it will make you stay longer than you planned to stay; and it will make you pay more than you had planned to pay.

We have counselled many couples whose marriages have been wrecked by outside interference from inside the living

## Letter of recommendation: people are not always what they seem

'Paul Jones, my assistant programmer, can always be found
hard at work in his cubicle. Paul works independently without
wasting company time talking to colleagues. Paul never
thinks twice about assisting fellow employees, and he always
finishes given assignments on time. Often Paul takes extended
measures to complete his work, sometimes skipping coffee
breaks. Paul is a single-minded individual who has absolutely no
vanity in spite of his high accomplishments and profound
knowledge in his field. I firmly believe that Paul can be
classed as a high-calibre employee, the type which cannot be
dispensed with. Consequently, I duly recommend that Paul be
promoted to executive management, and a proposal will be
sent away as soon as possible.'

A fax was sent soon afterwards which read: 'That incompetent employee was reading over my shoulder when I wrote the report sent to you earlier today. Kindly read every second line (i.e. 1, 3, 5, 7 etc) for my true assessment of him.'

room – pornography and dating on the computer. So many have told us they just began it as a joke – or out of boredom.

One person wrote, 'I am a Christian wife who has been devastated by my husband's involvement in Internet pornography. It is a miracle that I was even able to discover his secret habit, but I thank God that it came to light, even though it was almost a year after it first started. Thankfully, through counselling, time and grace from God, we have been able to work things out, but of course not without a great deal of tears, pain and regret.'

Singles, it's all right to meet friends on the computer, but make sure you know the values of the person to whom you are talking. In 1 Samuel 16:7 God says, ' "Don't judge by a man's face or height, for this is not the one. I don't make decisions the way you do! Men judge by outward appearance, but I look at a man's thoughts and intentions." '

## Purpose of premarital counselling

Some people ask, Do I really *need* premarital counselling? In times gone by, couples stayed together simply because of their vows. Not any more. Today, if people are not satisfied, they move on. Premarital counselling attempts to examine a couple's reasons for marriage and their understanding of love and commitment. It provides an opportunity for a couple to discuss vital components of a marriage, not simply a wedding.

Premarital counselling confronts idealistic and unrealistic expectations regarding marriage. It allows a couple to examine not only their present predicament and future plans but also family patterns of past generations.

Finally, premarital counselling facilitates a close bond between premarital counsellor and couple so that in the event of marital difficulties the couple may feel comfortable in seeking counsel. This is perhaps the most important reason, particularly as many ministers may concur with Cecil Osborne, who said of premarital couples in his book, *The Art of*

*Understanding Your Mate*, 'They tended to look at me through star dust, with amused tolerance.'

Especially in the absence of an extended family, premarital counselling is a necessity. *Ministers should not perform weddings for couples who have had no premarital counselling and who do not agree to go to counselling if their marriage should run into trouble.*

## Preparing for marriage?
## Then ask yourself these questions!

* How sacred is the marriage covenant to you?
* What is the attitude towards your proposed marriage of a) your parents, b) your friends, c) your future in-laws?
* How long have you courted?
* What differences are there in your social, economic, or cultural backgrounds?
* Do you have any disability or sexual dysfunction unknown to your fiancé/fiancee?
* How do you plan to manage your money? Do you have different views on money management?
* List the activities or interests outside the home that you have in common.
* How have you worked out the physical demonstrations of affection between yourselves? How about the non-physical demonstrations of affection?
* How do you resolve disagreements and differences of opinions?
* Why do people marry?
* Cite at least three reasons why you are marrying her/him.
* How confident are you that your proposed marriage is based on 'true love'?
* Why is marriage the beginning and not the end of love?
* List some key problems that may develop in marriage.

## Are you ready?

As you contemplate your own life, there may be things that you want to discover, develop and determine. Tick as appropriate; Yes **(Y)**, No **(N)**, Usually **(U)**.

| | Y | N | U |
|---|---|---|---|
| ● Firstly, ***discover***. Do you: | | | |
| * have confidence in your general ability to deal with failures and setbacks? | | | |
| * take it more or less for granted that people are interested in you and value you? | | | |
| * avoid worrying about tomorrow or fussing over yesterday's or today's mistakes? | | | |

| | | | |
|---|---|---|---|
| ● Secondly, ***develop***. Do you: | | | |
| * avoid excessive daydreaming and fantasy living ('if only I were a little taller. . .')? | | | |
| * 'keep on keeping on' even when you are discouraged, realizing that one step at | | | |
| a time in the right direction is enough? | | | |
| * see and consider the needs of others? | | | |

| | | | |
|---|---|---|---|
| ● Thirdly, ***determine***. Are you: | | | |
| * giving, forgiving, and full of thanksgiving? | | | |
| * interdependent, vulnerable, and empathetic? | | | |
| * open to finding love *right where you are?* | | | |
| * praying to *be* the right person as well as *find* the right person? | | | |

If your answers to most of the questions above are 'yes' or 'usually,' you are on the right track. If you are looking for a partner, look for a partner who is living a fulfilled life, not a frustrated one. Many marriages get off to the wrong start because they are simply the union of two frustrated singles more concerned about what they want *from* the relationship rather than what they can give *to* the relationship. Halsey Peat says, 'If your love revolves around your happiness, your desires, your ambitions, and your partner is an appendage to your happiness, then you only love yourself and should not marry.' And make no mistake about it – God will give His best to you.

# Love letter from God

Dear young people,

We are now in the twenty-first century and the end of the world is near. Many of you who love my Son are looking forward to His coming back to Earth. That makes me very happy. You are saying with my servant John, 'Come, Lord Jesus!' (Revelation 22:20).

There is something else, however, that many of you are hoping for. There is someone else that many of you are praying to see. In fact, I understand that you would like to see this person, if possible, before you see my Son. It is that special individual who will love and cherish you, whom you also will love and cherish.

It is all right to want the love of a human companion. It was I who placed that desire in your heart from the beginning. Do not be embarrassed or ashamed for what your heart desires. My servant Solomon said, 'The man who finds a wife finds a good thing; she is a blessing to him from the Lord' (Proverbs 18:22). Love is a good thing – as long as you remember that it is also a God-thing. It came from me; it must flow to me.

You see, I *am* love. It pleases me to see young people in love. When other people don't seem to understand you, remember *I* do.

You are young, so enjoy life. I created it for you. 'Don't let the excitement of being young cause you to forget about your Creator' (Ecclesiastes 12:1). Every day of life is a gift from me. Live it to the full – its blessings are only a foretaste of what is to come. 'It is a wonderful thing to be alive! If a person lives to be very old, let him rejoice in every day of life, but let him also remember that eternity is far longer' (11:8). I don't want to spoil your fun; I just don't want your fun to be spoiled. So 'let there be no sexual sin, impurity or greed among you. Let no one be able to accuse you of any such things. Dirty stories, foul talk and coarse jokes – these are not for you' (Ephesians 5:3,4). I just want you to have the best.

Two questions seem regularly to occupy the hearts of my young people. The first is: What should I look for in a boyfriend or girlfriend, a future husband or wife? The second question is: *Is there anyone out there for me?*

Let us look at your questions – ladies first.

Ladies, look for someone who is kind. 'Kindness makes a man attractive' (Proverbs 19:22). Have you discovered that? Watch how he treats his mother, his father – his sisters! It will show you something of how he may treat you. My servant Solomon said, 'A son who mistreats his father or mother is a public disgrace' (Proverbs 19:26). Don't be quickly taken in by his charming smile or the parting in his hair. It's not whether his parting is right, it's whether his heart is right. You can fix up a man's clothes, but you can't fix up his heart. Over time his life will reveal if his heart is right. Don't expect a heart that is not given over to me to treat you the way you want to be treated. 'A man is known by his actions. An evil man lives an evil life; a good man lives a godly life' (Proverbs 21:8).

Men, look for someone who is motivated to serve others. Some may want to look good in their earrings and necklaces, but look for someone who is more concerned about their Maker than their mirror. My servant Peter said, 'Don't be concerned about the outward beauty that depends on jewellery, or beautiful clothes, or hair arrangement. Be beautiful inside, in your hearts, with the lasting charm of a gentle and quiet spirit which is so precious to God' (1 Peter 3:3, 4). Solomon put it like this: 'Good sense is far more valuable than gold or precious jewels' (Proverbs 20:15).

So men, do not compare a Christian woman to a non-Christian woman using outward appearance as your only guide. The Christian woman has something you will be eternally grateful for; that is, unconditional love. 'Charm can be deceptive and beauty doesn't last, but a woman who fears and reverences God shall be greatly praised' (Proverbs 31:30).

My children, I beg you to change your perspective on love. Listen to your parents, elders, teachers, and fellow believers. Above all, make sure your guide is the Holy Word, not Hollywood. You smile, my child, but there are so many myths that come out of that false source. Some of them are:

* Romantic feelings are the best test in choosing a mate.
* Physical and emotional attraction can measure a relationship's intimacy.
* Living together is a good check for compatibility.
* God will protect you from the painful consequences of bad choices.

These are myths, my children! You need a wisdom beyond your years to choose wisely. Remember that true love is not based on *finding* the right person, but on *being* the right person. Change your perspective and continue to develop yourself.

It was I who said, 'It isn't good for man to be alone' (Genesis 2:18). Some have not understood. I desire first of all that you be in union with Me; and secondly, that you be in union with fellow believers. From this fellowship marriage may develop, but remember my child, your happiness consists not so much in marrying the person who may make you happy, but in escaping the many who can make you miserable!

Some of you have become disillusioned with marriage. You have seen your parents divorce. You have seen your brothers and sisters divorce. You have seen your friends marry and you have seen them divorce. Some of you have thought, perhaps it is better not to marry. I want you to know it was I who created marriage. I did it for two reasons. I wanted you to be happy with a human companion; but the second reason brings a tear to my eye. I wanted your marriage to be a constant reminder of how much my Son really loved you, by dying for you. My servant Paul understood this when he said, 'Husbands, show the same kind of love to your wives as Christ showed to the church when he died for her' (Ephesians 5:25). That is why your marriage vow says, 'Till death us do part.' And your marriage vow does not say, 'As long as *love* shall last' but rather, 'As long as *life* shall last'. So understand, if you choose to marry, it's a lifelong commitment – look before you leap!

*Young man:* 'Honour your marriage and its vows, and be pure; for God will surely punish all those who are immoral or commit adultery' (Hebrews 13:4).

*Young lady:* 'The wife is part of her husband as long as he lives' (1 Corinthians 7:39). It is because Jesus has promised that He's going to stay with you, that you can promise to stay with him. 'Be sure of this – that I am with you always, even to the end of the world' (Matthew 28:20).

Remember then, as Paul said, 'I'm not saying you *must* marry; but you certainly *may* if you wish' (1 Corinthians 7:6). Should you choose to marry, consider your time together as a gift, and value it. If the scythe of accident or sickness robs you of your loved one, consider the time you spent together as a gift, and treasure it. Should you choose not to marry – or should a companion not be a present reality – then consider your time while single as a gift and nurture it. 'God gives some the gift of a husband or wife, and others he gives the gift of being able to stay happily unmarried' (1 Corinthians 7:7).

And so to your last question: Is he out there at all? Is she out there? my answer is: perhaps. I know that may not be satisfactory for you, but it is all you can take for now. Do not let romance consume your life. Keep your eyes open and respect yourself. There needs to be more analysis and less romance *before* marriage and more romance and less analysis *after* marriage.

Love your parents. Love your sisters and brothers in the Lord. Love me and love life. Keep sex for your marriage, for sex is my wedding gift to every married couple, and it is a gift I don't want you to open early. Be positive, not pessimistic; cheerful, not critical; motivated, not mournful. And when those times come when you feel that you've hit rock bottom, remember – I made the rock.

*Your loving Father*

P.S. 'There are "friends" who pretend to be friends, but there is a friend who sticks closer than a brother' (Proverbs 18:24). That Friend is my Son. But of course, you knew that!

Love your parents. Love your sisters and brothers in the Lord. Love me and love life.

## Solowork on Chapter 3

# Love - The Real Deal

Answer each question truthfully regardless of what another person wants to hear!

| | | YES | NO |
|---|---|---|---|
| **1.** | Do you and your friend have many interests in common? | | |
| **2.** | Do you have a feeling of pride when you compare your friend to any other you have known? | | |
| **3.** | Do you feel you need to apologize for certain things about her/him? | | |
| **4.** | Do you suffer from a feeling of unrest when away from her/him? | | |
| **5.** | Have you a strong desire to please your companion, and are you quite glad to give way on your own preference? | | |
| **6.** | Do you have any difficulty carrying on a conversation with each other? | | |
| **7.** | Even when you quarrel do you still enjoy being together? | | |
| **8.** | Do you actually want to marry this person? | | |
| **9.** | Would you be afraid to trust her/him in the presence of another attractive person of your own sex for an evening? | | |
| **10.** | Does she/he have the qualities you would like to have in your children? | | |
| **11.** | Do your friends and associates admire this person and think that he or she would be a good match for you? | | |
| **12.** | Do you ever wonder if your friend is faithful to you? | | |
| **13.** | Do your parents think you are in love? | | |
| **14.** | Have you started planning, at least in your own mind, what kind of wedding and home to have? What about children? | | |
| **15.** | Is your companion attractive to you not only in appearance but in the way they talk, act and think? | | |
| **16.** | Do you approve generally of each other's friends? | | |
| **17.** | Do you wonder if your friend is being sincere in what they tell you? | | |

| continued: | | YES | NO |
|---|---|---|---|
| **18.** | Do you have a wealth of things to discuss and do together? | | |
| **19.** | Do you find that in thinking of the future it is always in terms of the two of you rather than just yourself? | | |
| **20.** | Can you imagine how she/he will appear in 20 years' time, and do you think you will still feel as deeply attached as now? | | |
| **21.** | When outside trouble develops for one of you, does the crisis tend to pull you together rather than apart? | | |
| **22.** | Are there many things on which you disagree? | | |
| **23.** | Are you conscious of being jealous of your companion? | | |
| **24.** | Do you have serious doubts about your love for your friend? | | |
| **25.** | Do you think your friend would make a good parent for your children? | | |
| **26.** | Do you approve of your friend's religion and philosophy of life? | | |

## How to score:

**Perfect score** – NO for questions 3, 6, 9, 12, 17, 22, 23, 24 and YES for all the rest.

**Solidly in love** – 23 or more 'correct' answers.

**Watch out** – 20-22 'correct' answers.

**Hold out!** – Fewer than 20.

## READ ON!

| Author | Book title | Publisher |
|---|---|---|
| Harris, Joshua | I Kissed Dating Goodbye | Multnomah Books |
| McCallum, D. & DeLashmutt, G. | The Myth of Romance | Bethany House |
| Williams, Richard | They Stole It, But You Must Return It | HEMA Publishing |

# Chapter 4

# It hurts so bad

Dear Dr Brown

What does a woman who is trying to be a Christian do when she feels the need for physical intimacy and companionship? In many ways I feel cheated. I believe I have been faithful to God to the best of my ability. God has said He will not withhold any good thing from us. I do not believe a companion is a bad thing. People say God may be preparing you and the person you will meet. This does not console me at all because I cannot live in the future. Now is what I have to contend with. Tomorrow is not promised to me.

When your needs aren't met, they become bigger. I have watched my need for companionship become bigger and bigger over the years, to the point where I became sexually active in an attempt to escape the prison of my loneliness, if only for a short while. I had always thought that I chose my actions. I had not been aware previously of the influence circumstance had on my choices. I never imagined that I would become sexually active before marriage.

Dr Brown, I feel God has neglected this aspect of my life; theoretically, I know this is not true as God is interested in the whole person. However, my reality suggests otherwise and my reality is what I have to live with.

It is painful for me to see couples, because I wish I could be part of a couple. I know not all couples have good relationships but I am tired, really tired, of being alone.

A very real fear is that if I meet someone I will be so needy of their companionship that I will push them away; although my being aware of this may help in some way.

People say, 'Be patient.' I find this insulting as I have been very patient. I cannot deny my humanity. I need companionship, intimacy and physical intimacy. I cannot pretend this need doesn't exist.

I have used up all my resources trying to cope with loneliness and I am so weak and fragile now. Time hasn't made me stronger, it has made me weak, very weak. I do not know why God has not provided me with a companion despite my begging. 'Ask and ye shall receive'. I certainly have not received. I must be interpreting this wrongly. I write hoping you may be able to help somehow, though I must admit, my hope has been worn thin.

Sarah

## No more sheets

Juanita Bynum electrified her audience as she spoke at a T. D. Jakes Ministries Singles' Convention on the subject, 'No More Sheets.' She said she is tired of hearing married folk telling single folks to 'hold on' while *they* are having all the sex they want. In her words, 'I want to hear "hold on" from someone who's *really* holding on!' Her point is taken. No wonder one songwriter said, 'It hurts so bad'.

Bynum makes the following points:

* Holding on is a struggle. If you are or

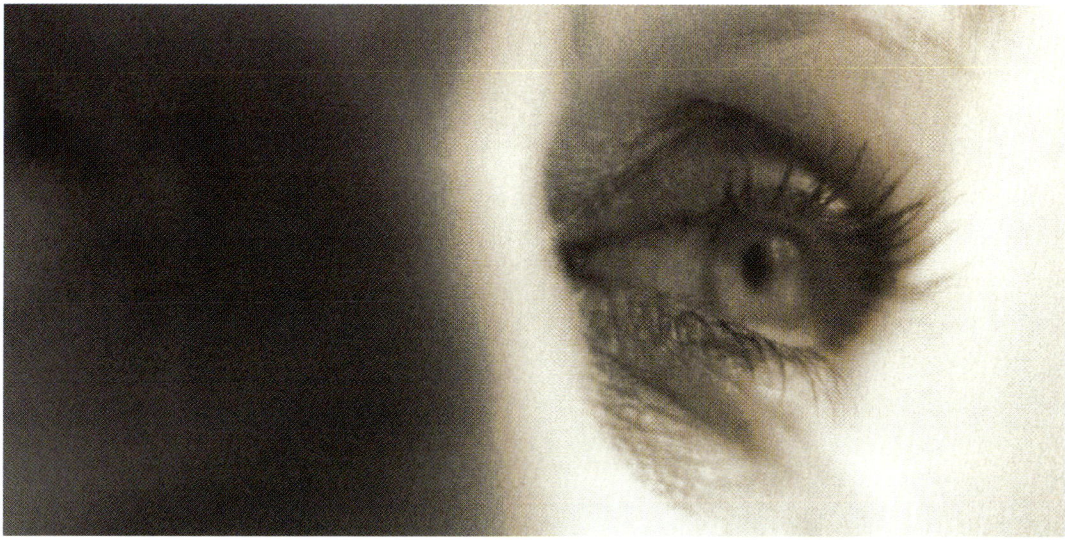

have been sexually active, breaking free and staying free is a struggle. And just when you think you have broken free, the devil uses your imagination to create an unrealistically erotic romantic encounter, and before you know it, you're back in the trap, back between the sheets again. But God wants to purify your mind. God wants to take you through a process whereby you allow Him to cleanse your body, your mind and your heart of past relationships, past hurts, past abuses. *God wants to put your body back together again.*

* Tell that friend of yours, 'I'm not ready for marriage. It's not you, it's me. I can't mess up your life.' You're not ready for marriage because you're not single yet. You are still attached to old boyfriends and old girlfriends, and past thrills from illicit sexual encounters, adult videos, pornography in magazines and on the internet. Marriage is not about sex, it's about ministry. 'Sex - it ain't everything. If you're not prepared to minister to the men and women of God, don't mess over them.'

* The way back will not be easy. You've got to walk in the depth of God until it supersedes the depth of sin that you've come from. Whatever it took you to get free, you've got to do that to stay free. If in order to get free you immersed yourself in the Scriptures, bathed yourself in prayer and surrounded yourself with wholesome Christian friends – then you've got to keep that up in order to stay free!

## Planning for victory

Where are these friends? Is there anyone who will say today, with Paul, 'And you should follow my example, just as I follow Christ's' (1 Corinthians 11:1)? Los Angeles Lakers basketball star A. C. Green has taken up the challenge. He was bold enough to tell the magazine *New Man:* 'I am a role model, look at me. If I can stay sexually pure, then you can too.'

On Dr James Dobson's radio programme, *Focus on the Family,* A. C. Green said, 'I want young people to hear this message: It is possible to wait. Not everybody is doing it. I'm proud to say that I am a virgin, and I don't hide the strength God has given me.'

In American football, to keep the other team from scoring late in the game, the team that's leading uses what is known as a 'prevent defence'. A. C. Green, in his book *Victory: Principles of Championship Living*, came up with five 'Prevent Defence Rules' that govern his life:

**1)** I don't feed my eyes on lustful images. I don't watch television and movies that show people having sex. I don't listen to music that tells me to have sex. The lower your exposure, the higher your tolerance grows.

**2)** I don't put myself in tempting situations. I don't invite a woman to my house at midnight to watch a movie or 'have a Bible study'. No one wants to be the party pooper, but you have to draw that line.

**3)** I have studied Proverbs 6. The adulterous woman is out to spoil me with flattering lips and seductive looks. It's a perfect picture painted by my enemy to get me to fall into his scene. You don't have to be a rocket scientist to figure it out.

**4)** I use the buddy system. I often have a third party with me instead of being alone with a woman. I'm not likely to make a pass if someone is right there watching me.

Having a group of like-minded friends to whom you are accountable is a great way to keep your feet on the ground.

**5)** I keep myself accountable to my friends. I've gone to Lee, Greg, Dave and others with egg all over my face more than once. Even though they love me unconditionally, I don't like telling them when I've failed. They are the pit crew to my race car, and they always get me back on track.

## Standing firm

Youth specialist Dr Baraka Muganda says, 'Young people who have principles have preferred to remain silent because, if they defend them, they are ridiculed. Today, our African youth require more valour to remain stable and steadfast than in the days of Shadrach, Meshach and Abednego. The temptations are many and

various. They need to say No, on a daily basis, to alcohol, tobacco and drugs. The lightness with which society regards sex makes it a real burden for each young person who must face it daily.'

## Teenage pregnancies

For college students on the career path, having a child just does not fit the picture. As Dr Lynda Smith Harris, a psychiatrist based in New York City, explains, 'I think people are realizing that it's not wise economically – it's not "upwardly mobile" – to have children before they're ready.'

Yet Dr Zacchaeus Mathema, university professor in Kenya, says that in one university almost 50 per cent of young women who enrol each year have their academic careers cut short or disturbed by premarital pregnancies. Something that

### Implications of early menarche

Early maturing girls are more likely to:

* become sexually active at an earlier age
* engage in sexually promiscuous behaviour during adolescence
* have more emotional problems such as depression and anxiety
* experience more conflict with their parents
* have an earlier first birth

Ludwig Werner Binemann

is becoming glaringly obvious is that girls *now become women much earlier than before.*

Over the past century, the age of menarche – a woman's first menstrual period – has declined at the rate of three to four months per decade in the Western world, paralleled by improvements in health, nutrition, sanitation and socio-economic conditions. Whereas in the mid-nineteenth century the average age was 17, currently the average age is 12.5.

In the mid-nineteenth century cognitive and physical maturity occurred nearly simultaneously. Now children are attaining physical maturity well in advance of the cognitive and intellectual maturity to cope with it. Over a century ago teen pregnancy was less common because menarche occurred late in teenage years and girls are not usually fertile until one or two years following menarche. Now adolescent pregnancy is a major national concern, especially in the United States with over one million teens a year becoming pregnant.

The upshot of all of this is that young people are experiencing sexual urges at an earlier time than ever before in history. Some have decided, however, that it's time to draw a line.

## Can you wait?

*True Love Waits* was started in the United States by the Southern Baptist Church. The idea was to encourage teenagers and young adults to keep themselves sexually for their future spouse; to start being faithful to their future partner now. One of their

mottos is, 'Don't be a louse. Wait for a spouse.' One July, over 200,000 pledge cards were fixed to the ground around Capitol Hill, Washington, representing young Americans who wanted to state publicly that they were ready to wait for marriage to have sex.

Why the sudden change and sudden interest? In Britain, one newspaper called it the latest 'fad'. It could be. But possibly it's because young people are beginning to realize that life need not revolve around sex. *Ebony* magazine allowed Greg and Tanya to speak for themselves.

## Our story

Greg Mooreland, 20, says, 'I'd been exploring my roots and wanted the discipline and community of an African organization. I felt that I could rise to higher levels, spiritually and mentally, if I wasn't so focused on sex.' Both Greg and Tanya think that celibacy has strengthened their relationship.

Greg says, 'My relationship with Tanya has grown deeper. When we were having sex, we didn't talk as much. Now that we're not having sex, we do more – we go out more often and we spend more time just talking.'

Tanya says, 'We've learned more about each other. We're clearer about why we want to be together because we've moved to a higher level. We communicate much better, we really listen to each other, and it's funny, we argue less.'

## Attraction

Zoologist and anthropologist Desmond Morris observed the bonding process across several cultures. He concluded, 'The progress from the first attraction to final trust is nearly always a long and complex sequence of gradually increasing intimacies.' For convenience, we can divide the human sequence up into twelve stages:

**1) Eye to body.** The process of visual stimulation where one person sees another and interest in knowing more about them is aroused.

**2) Eye to eye.** The process of eye contact, where the eyes meet and the look of interest is reciprocated. Make no mistake, some people have very powerful eyes!

**3) Voice to voice.** The process of verbal communication where individuals look for every opportunity to talk.

**4) Hand to hand.** The process of touch, more than formalized or helping-hand contact. As the relationship develops, hand-holding or arm-holding becomes prolonged.

**5) Arm to shoulder.** The first encircling gesture, signifying that a special relationship has developed.

**6) Arm to waist.** This physical closeness signals a deepening investment in each other, a growing trust and confidence.

**7) Face to face or mouth to mouth.** The two now turn face to face and intense self-disclosure begins. Friendship bonding has given way to pair-bonding. There is a strong chance of physiological arousal if the action is prolonged or repeated.

**8) Hand to head.** The hands begin to caress the partner's head. This represents deepening levels of trust and unconditional acceptance.

**9) Hand to body** (not sexually directed). There is an increasingly comfortable level of giving and receiving touch. We become more comfortable with revealing who we are inside and further physiological arousal takes place.

**10 to 12) Mouth to breast, Hands to genitals, Genitals to genitals.** These final stages lead to the full intimacy of sexual intercourse, and there are inevitable and irreversible biological, emotional, social and philosophical consequences.

## No Rush

'When steps are missed in the rush to genital intimacy, the bond tends to be deformed and to break. A person who has reached genital intimacy in one relationship tends to move even more quickly to genital intimacy almost immediately in any future relationships, just to find that sexual experience which is not well grounded in extended and shared life experience through light touching and long conversation. Premature direct genital contact will foreclose completion of the bonding process for months or years to come.'

Donald Joy, *Bonding: Relationships in the Image of God.*

## It's downhill from here!

Think of these stages as if you were in a truck going downhill. As you move from one stage to the next, the truck picks up speed. You plan to apply the brakes soon, but you just want to experience the next stage, then you'll stop. The next stage is so sweet that you want to experience the stage after that. When you try to apply the brakes the truck is travelling so fast that by then, *once you have passed a certain point, it becomes extremely hard to stop the truck with all the good will in the world.*

I read something once called *A Little Music for the Road:*

'At 45 miles per hour it's "God will take care of you".

'At 55 mph, "Guide me, O Thou Great Jehovah".

'At 65 mph, "Nearer my God to Thee".

'At 75mph, "Nearer, still nearer!".

'At 85 mph, "This world is not my home".

'At 95 mph, "Lord, I'm coming home".

'Over 100mph, "Precious memories".'

## Damaged goods

Yes, speed can have serious consequences! But consider two pieces of balsa wood. Coat them with super-glue. Press them together and pull them apart immediately. Very little damage is done. That is how it is when your relationship breaks up in stages 1-3. Keep the balsa wood together for an extended period of time and then try to separate the two pieces. They can be separated, but *they cannot be separated without severe damage being done to both surfaces of wood.* That's stages 10-12.

## Too soon to celebrate?

You're not supposed to break up once you enter those stages. You see, those stages are meant for marriage only. Stephen Grunlan, in *Marriage and the Family: A Christian Perspective,* outlines the levels of intimate activities (see bar at the bottom of page).

Grunlan says, 'Rather than engage in every permissible behaviour early in their relationship, they ought to save various expressions of physical intimacy to celebrate various stages of their relationship.'

It is for you to discuss how far is too far with your partner. Many couples exclaim, 'Oh, we know so much about each other!' What they really mean is, we know all the contours of the body, BUT –

What about her physical health?
What about his spiritual commitment?
What about his family history?
What about her educational interests?
*What do you really know?*

### Key:

**L** – Look
**T** – Touch (casual embrace)
**h** – Occasional holding hands
**H** – Constant holding hands
**k** – Light kiss
**K** – Strong kiss
**fK** – French kiss
**B** – Fondling of breasts
**SO** – Sexual organs (foreplay)
**SI** – Sexual intercourse

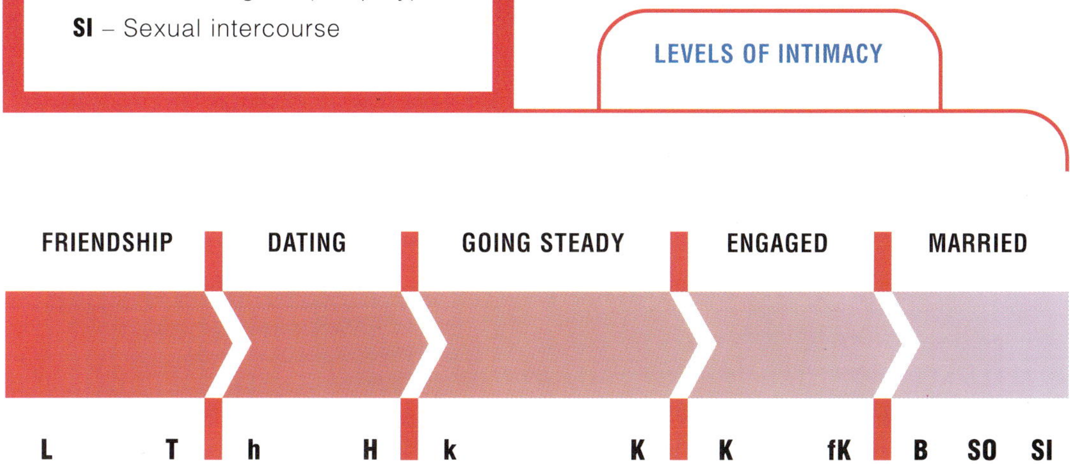

## Moonstruck?

The time for you to discuss how far is too far is not when the moon is up in the sky, but when the sun is up in the sky. Not when you are in the back seat of the car but when you are on the park bench – and the little old lady is walking past you.

## How did we let it get this far?

Remember that when physical intimacy increases, verbal communication shuts down. I'm just trying to say that *the best time to talk about where to draw the line with physical intimacy is when you are not surrounded by temptation!*

Staying up late at night in solitary proximity with a member of the opposite sex is almost guaranteed to end in physical intimacy. Take it from me. We ministers have heard it all: 'Oh, pastor, we were just doing our Bible study. I don't know how it happened.' *Well, we know!*

## Hands-off courtship?

'We are aware that the idea that couples go through a courtship with little or no caressing seems out of touch with reality,' say Dave and Joyce Ames in their book *Looking Up the Aisle.* 'By this point in the relationship almost any kiss, with the possible exception of a peck on the cheek, becomes a transmitter of sexual messages. A lot of couples involved with our singles ministry have taken the challenge of "hands-off" courting and have since thanked us for it, even though at the time they wondered if they could not get by with something a bit less conservative.'

## Try before you buy?

The question is asked by some, shouldn't you test the merchandise before you buy? My answer is, *test the mind* – and the body will take care of itself!

I like how the Ames put it: 'Physical intimacy promises to seal and secure the relationship, but this is a deception. Relationships become secure only when we know our partner and we are known by

## Sexual Abuse

In an age of rampant sexual abuse, there are some pains whose hurt goes very deep. Answer below according to what you really believe yourself, not what you think you should believe, true (**T**) or untrue (**U**). The value of this lies in your openness. Remember, it is never the victim's fault – you are still a child of God, with incredible attractiveness and inestimable worth.

| BELIEF | T | U |
|---|---|---|
| **1)** I must be an extremely rare woman to have experienced sex with an older person when I was a child. | | |
| **2)** I am worthless and bad. | | |
| **3)** You can't depend on women; they are all weak and useless creatures. | | |
| **4)** No man can be trusted. | | |
| **5)** I must have permitted sex to happen because I wasn't forced into it. | | |
| **6)** I don't have the right to deny my body to any man who demands it. | | |
| **7)** Anyone who knows what happened to me sexually will not want anything to do with me. | | |
| **8)** I must have been seductive and provocative when I was young. | | |
| **9)** It doesn't matter what happens to me in my life. | | |
| **10)** No man could care for me without a sexual relationship. | | |
| **11)** It is dangerous to get close to anyone because they always betray, exploit or hurt you. | | |
| **12)** I must have been responsible for the sex when I was young because it went on so long. | | |
| **13)** I will never be able to lead a normal life; the damage is permanent. | | |
| **14)** Only bad, worthless men would be interested in me. | | |
| **15)** It must be unnatural to feel any pleasure during molestation. | | |
| **16)** I am inferior to other people because I did not have normal experiences. | | |
| **17)** I've already been used so it doesn't matter if other men use me. | | |
| **18)** I was responsible for the abuse because I asked the offender about sexual matters. | | |
| **19)** The offender abused me because he was 'sick' and therefore not responsible for his actions. | | |
| **20)** The abuse was my own fault because I used sexual activities to gain attention and/or affection from the offender. | | |

*Continued*

| BELIEF | T | U |
|---|---|---|
| **21)** The offender abused me because he was drunk at the time. | | |
| **22)** I was to blame for the abuse because I used it to obtain favours and rewards from the offender. | | |
| **23)** The offender abused me because he was sexually frustrated. | | |
| **24)** The offender engaged me in sexual activities in order to make me a better sexual partner. | | |
| **25)** The offender engaged in sexual activities with me so that our physical and/or social relationship would be closer and better. | | |

them. This is the objective of courtship. *We can trust God that all of the other equipment will function as advertised.'*

## Sex – satisfaction or frustration?

Several years ago researchers at the University of Chicago released the results of the most 'comprehensive and methodologically sound' sex survey ever conducted. Their findings surprised many people: *religious women experience significantly higher levels of sexual satisfaction than non-religious women.* This was not the first study that showed a link between spirituality and sexuality.

## Enduring marital sex or enjoying it?

In 1970, *Redbook* magazine published the findings of a Sexual Pleasure Survey, written by Robert Levin, co-author – with Masters and Johnson – of *The Pleasure Bond.* This survey showed the preferences of 100,000 women. Listed first was that 'sexual satisfaction is related significantly to religious belief. With notable consistency, the greater the intensity of a woman's religious convictions, the likelier she is to be highly satisfied with the sexual pleasures of marriage.'

The story has gone around that Christians are sexually repressed. They're so used to not being allowed to do it that when marriage comes and it's all right to do it, they can't do it, or if they do, they don't enjoy it! They want to do it, but they're not supposed to, so they just think about it, then someone comes along and says if you've thought about it it's the same as actually doing it, so some conclude they might as well do it then and get some fun out of it. But the script has been written wrong!

But why are religious women more satisfied sexually? Four reasons:

## Inexperienced? That's *good!*

**Firstly,** religious women appear to benefit from their lack of sexual experience prior to marriage. Yes! Several studies, including the *Redbook* survey, show that women who engage in early sexual activity and those who have had multiple partners are less apt to express satisfaction with their sex lives than women who entered marriage with little or no sexual baggage.

## No fear, no guilt, no wonder

**Thirdly,** religious people typically enjoy greater sexual freedom – watch out! A 1982 University of California (Los Angeles) study found that sexual satisfaction is positively affected by 'the absence of sexual anxiety'. Part of the reason why religious people have more fun is that they don't have to worry about many of the fears commonly associated with sexual promiscuity:

* AIDS;
* Other sexually-transmitted diseases;
* Fear of rejection;
* Fear of out-of-wedlock pregnancy;
* Fear of getting caught.

Religious people also tend to be free from the guilt associated with violating their own sexual standards. A University of

**Secondly,** religious people seem to benefit from a commitment to marital fidelity and marital permanence. David Larson, of the National Institute for Healthcare Research reports, 'Couples not involved before marriage and faithful during marriage appear to be more satisfied with their current sex life than those who were involved sexually before marriage.'

## Sexual restraint – easy or hard?

'Christian sexual standards actually make it easier, rather than more difficult, for single men and women to share genuine friendship without fear of exploitation. High moral standards nullify ulterior motives and allow single women to have greater confidence that they're being appreciated as persons rather than sex objects.'

W. Peter Blitchington, *The Christian Woman's Search for Self-Esteem.*

Connecticut study found this guilt to be a hindrance to sexual satisfaction among unmarried college students.

## It's God's idea

**Fourthly,** religious people appear to benefit from the belief that God created sex. It was Solomon who said, 'There is nothing new under the sun.' A wise person will learn from those who have gone before them. The 1960s was a period of rebellion and revolution which promised sexual freedom to all its supporters.

Twenty years later the cover story of *Time* magazine would read, 'The sex revolution is over.' In seven pages of close-packed copy, the authors concluded: 'Veterans of the revolution, some wounded, some merely bored, are re-inventing courtship and romance and discovering, often with astonishment, that they need not sleep together on the first or second date. Many individuals are even rediscovering the traditional values of fidelity, obligation and marriage', – (9 April, 1984).

## AIDS

Mae Williams, a 21-year-old college senior, has noticed that AIDS has changed the rules of sexual pursuit among people she knows at Howard University. Mae, a virgin, says candidly, 'Look, this is not the sixties when there was all that free love. I know this to be true – a lot of students aren't having sex and aren't ashamed to say so. AIDS scares all of us.'

Tragically, the greatest number of patients with HIV infection is in the developing countries, particularly in the rural areas where resources are few. The hope

## Our only hope

'HIV/AIDS is a serious problem in the world in general and in Africa in particular. Many people want to change the world, but few want a change in lifestyle. What we need is not a new suit for every African man. Rather, what we need is a new man inside every suit! Nay, not a new dress for every African woman, but a new woman inside every dress. What we need are changed habits and conduct; a changed society is the only way out of the dilemma the HIV/AIDS epidemic has put us into. This is an insistent imperative, and it is our only hope.'

Dr Paul Wangai, Jun.

for Africa rests largely in prevention of HIV infection. Dr Paul Wangai, Jun, in an African Christian journal, looks at family life today and laments: 'Our African cultures are disintegrating as we embrace Western patterns in all areas [dress, diet, behaviour, beliefs, norms]. As a result, we have hitherto unknown crises of divorce, illicit sex, separation, domestic violence, incest and many others, which in many cultures were a taboo [some punishable by death].'

## What about abstinence?

I was holding a notice from my 13-year-old son's school announcing a meeting to preview the new course in sexuality. Parents could examine the curriculum and take part in an actual lesson presented exactly as it would be given to the students. When I arrived at the school, I was surprised to discover only about a dozen parents there. As we waited for the presentation, I thumbed through page after page of instructions in the prevention of pregnancy or disease. I found abstinence mentioned only in passing.

When the teacher arrived with the school nurse, she asked if there were any questions. I asked why abstinence did not play a noticeable part in the material. What happened next was shocking. There was a great deal of laughter, and someone suggested that if I thought abstinence had any merit, I should go back to burying my head in the sand.

The teacher and the nurse said nothing as I drowned in a sea of embarrassment. My mind had gone blank, and I could think of nothing to say. The teacher explained to me that the job of the school was to teach 'facts', and the home was responsible for moral training. I sat in silence for the next twenty minutes as the course was explained.

The other parents seemed to give their unqualified support to the materials. 'Doughnuts at the back,' announced the teacher during the break.

'I'd like you to put on the name tags we have prepared – they're right by the doughnuts – and mingle with the other parents.'

Everyone moved to the back of the room.

As I watched them affixing their name tags and shaking hands, I sat deep in thought. I was ashamed that I had not been able to convince them to include a serious discussion of abstinence in the materials. I uttered a silent prayer for guidance. My thoughts were interrupted

If our hope is not in Hollywood, it must be in the Church and community agencies. While the Church desires to be a hospital for sick sinners, in practice it is sometimes not as compassionate as it claims to be. One church decided to

by Robert Layton

by the teacher's hand on my shoulder. 'Won't you join the others, Mr Layton?' The nurse smiled sweetly at me. 'The dough-nuts are good.' 'Thank you, no,' I replied.

'Well, then, how about a name tag? I'm sure the others would like to meet you.' 'Somehow I doubt that,' I replied. 'Won't you please join them?' she coaxed. Then I heard a still, small voice whisper, 'Don't go.' The instruction was unmistakable. 'I'll just wait here,' I said.

When the class was called back to order, the teacher looked around the long table and thanked everyone for putting on name tags. She ignored me. Then she said, 'Now we're going to give you the same lesson we'll be giving your children. Everyone please peel off your name tags.' I watched in silence as the tags came off. 'On the back of one of the tags, I drew a tiny flower. Who has it, please?'

The gentleman across from me held it up. 'Here it is!' 'All right,' she said. 'The flower represents disease. Do you recall with whom you shook hands?' He pointed to a couple of people. 'Very good,' she replied. 'The handshake in this case represents intimacy. So the two people you had contact with now have the disease.' There was laughter and joking among the parents.

The teacher continued, 'And with whom did the two of you shake hands?' The point was well taken, and she explained how this lesson would show students how quickly disease is spread. 'Since we all shook hands, we all have the disease.'

It was then that I heard the still, small voice again. 'Speak now', it said, 'but be humble.' I noted wryly the latter admon-ition, then rose from my chair. I apologized for any upset I might have caused earlier, congratulated the teacher on an excellent lesson that would impress the youth, and concluded by saying I had only one small point I wished to make.

'Not all of us were infected,' I said. 'One of us – abstained.'

change that and declared: 'The Christ-like response to AIDS must be personal – compassionate, helpful, and redemptive. Just as Jesus cared about those with leprosy, the feared communicable disease of His day, His followers today will care for those with AIDS.'

## Emergency! Calling all 'God-fearers'

In addition to compassion, there must be dialogue with community agencies and 'God-fearers'. It is good to see calls for all who desire healthiness in human relations according to God's standard to come together and join forces against the common enemies, such as AIDS.

Dr Michael Anderson, an expert on the sociology of religion, states in an African journal of religion: 'Dialogue among "God-fearers" is a necessity in our present age of interconnectedness. It should take place with the aim to deepen understanding and insight between each other. By so doing, as religions of the world we present ourselves with a golden opportunity to reveal to our societies and to the world at large, a more accurate and collective description of the character of God in whom our faith resides and His relevance

### No consequences?

'It is interesting that the entertainment industry, including television producers, are wringing their hands about this terrible epidemic of AIDS. They profess to be very concerned about those who are infected with sexually-transmitted diseases, and perhaps they are sincere. However, television executives and movie moguls have contributed mightily to the existence of this plague.

'For decades, they have depicted teens and young adults climbing in and out of each other's beds like so many sexual robots. Only the nerds were shown to be chaste, and they were too stupid or ugly to find partners. Of course, the beautiful young actors in those steamy dramas never faced any consequences for their sexual indulgence.

'No one ever came down with herpes or syphillis, or chlamydia, or pelvic inflammatory disease, or infertility, or AIDS, or genital warts, or cervical cancer.'

Dr James Dobson, A Message from *Focus on the Family.*

in and to our world today.' If we are going to beat this evil scourge called AIDS, we need all hands on deck. Let each of us make ourself a committee of one to keep ourself pure and to help those who stand in need.

## Jesus is the answer

'And so, dear brothers [and sisters], I plead with you to give your bodies to God. Let them be a living sacrifice, holy – the kind he can accept. When you think of what he has done for you, is this too much to ask?' (Romans 12:1). The Bible tells you how to avoid falling, but the Bible also shares what Dr E. E. Cleveland calls, 'the theology of recovery: in simple language, how to bounce back.'

Don't let anybody tell you you've gone too far to turn around. Jesus went all the way to the cross because some of us have gone all the way. Ellen White says in the book, *The Ministry of Healing,* page 229; 'He knows each individual by name, and cares for each as if there were not another upon the earth for whom He gave His beloved Son.' There is forgiveness, there is healing, there is reconciliation – all at the foot of the cross.

Reader, be honest with your situation! These are desperate times that we are living in! You can fool some of the people all of the time, and you can even fool yourself some of the time, but you can't fool God *any* of the time. 1 John 1:8-9 says, 'If we say that we have no sin, we are only fooling ourselves, and refusing to accept the truth. But if we confess our sins to him, he can be depended on to forgive us and to cleanse us from every wrong. And it is perfectly proper for God to do this for us because Christ died to wash away our sins.'

Young people, you who are caught up in film stars and sports stars, there's only one star in the

great drama of life and that is not Jesus Christ Superstar, it's Jesus Christ the bright and morning star. Catherine Marshall, in *We Walk in Wistfulness* says, 'The single person suspects – probably rightly – that there is no final perfect solution to the physical problem for the unmarried person.' I want to suggest to you a final perfect solution – His name is Jesus. There is no better answer.

## Solowork on Chapter 4

### Sex, lies and . . .

Cora is a beautiful island maiden. She and Hector are in love. They live on two Caribbean islands which are very close together, but separated by a sea which is full of sharks. Hector rows over in his dinghy to visit Cora every day. One day he does not come. He sends a message that he is seriously ill. His message implores Cora to come and visit him and bring medicine, but she has no way to cross the shark-infested sea that separates their islands.

Cora gets the medicine and asks Captain Hook, the ferry-boat driver, to take her over to Hector. Captain Hook says that he will be glad to, but he wants Cora to exchange her 'favours' for the ride. She refuses.

Cora then goes to Fisherman Fred whom she knows has a boat. Fred refuses to get involved, so Cora, having exhausted all other possibilities, returns to the Captain and meets the conditions of passage.

She delivers the medicine to Hector and tells him the saga of her trip. Hector recovers in due time, but can no longer love Cora because of her indiscretion with the Captain. Heartbroken, Cora cries on the shoulder of Bluto. Bluto is enraged at the unfairness. He has a fisticuffs with Hector. Hector is definitely on the losing end of the fight. He loses a mouthful of teeth and sustains a black eye.

News of Hector's woes reaches Cora. She is delighted at Hector's bad luck. She thinks he got what he deserves and has a good laugh at his expense.

In your opinion, *who was the worst*

## Choosing to stop

'Even teens who have been sexually active can choose to stop. This is often called "secondary virginity", a good concept that conveys the idea that kids can start over. One young girl wrote to Ann Landers to say she wished she had kept her virginity, signing the letter, "Sorry I didn't and wish I could take it back." As responsible adults we need to tell her that even though she can't go back, she can go forward. She can regain her self-respect and protect her health, because it's never too late to start saying "no" to premarital sex.'

Dr James Dobson, *Focus on the Family.*

*character in the story?* Give that person the number 1. Give the best person the number 5 and fill in the in-between. Loyalty, commitment, trust, betrayal, abuse, sexual faithfulness – what other themes come to mind? Why not talk it through with some friends? Have fun!

| | |
|---|---|
| **Hector** | |
| **Cora** | |
| **Fisherman Fred** | |
| **Captain Hook** | |
| **Bluto** | |

## READ ON!

| Author | Book title | Publisher |
|---|---|---|
| Gregory, Ian Stuart | No Sex Please, We're Single | Kingsway |
| Jones, Alfred R. & Jones, Doris E. | A Door of Hope for the Wounded Black Family | Family Outreach Publications |
| Miles, Herbert J. | Singles, Sex & Marriage | Word |

# Chapter 5

# All by myself

Dearest Browns

This letter has taken approximately one year to write. I'm sure you both remember that I went to Bermuda. Jeff, you were absolutely right, it's a country full of natural beauty and simply delightful people! One slight hiccup: where were all the single Christian men? None to be found on this occasion, although I was assured that there were a lot of students away studying.

So I came back to England still praying and seeking a partner but saying to myself God will provide in time. Six years ago I met a man at a friend's wedding, we got to know each other and became good friends. He is not a Christian but he has Christian friends. To cut a long story short, we started to see a lot more of each other and we officially started dating.

I made it quite clear that I would not marry someone unless he is a believer of my faith but on the other hand I did not want him to come to the Lord for my sake, but for his own. He is a very warm, caring and loving person who I feel is sent from heaven and in terms of spirituality, he demonstrates a Christian nature.

My dilemma now is that he needs to receive Bible studies. He has started to attend church with me in London, but he has a lot of unanswered questions. He is quite intellectual and sometimes feels that he is given wishy-washy answers to his questions. It is clear that he needs to be grounded in the fundamentals in order for him firstly to build a personal relationship with God, and secondly so that he can understand me better.

Joseph desperately needs someone to study with and what better and more trusting person could I think of than you, Jeff. Please let me know your thoughts about Joseph and perhaps developing a study programme for him.

Sharon

## Have you checked the baggage?

Don't you just hate those airport questions: 'Have you packed the bags yourself? Have the bags always been in your sight? Could anybody have put anything in that you are unaware of?' Time-consuming questions – but questions designed to save somebody's life.

Marriage is about baggage. You have baggage and the person you marry has baggage. When people tell you, 'She looks good', or 'He will treat you well', or 'You won't get much better than that', the real question is, *have you checked the baggage yourself?* It may just save your life.

## Life and death

Mary was a lovely young lady who grew up in a Christian home. She asked me if I would pay a visit to her house and meet her husband. I did. It was there that I heard a story that almost made me weep. Mary had married Peter ten years earlier. He was not a Christian, but he loved Mary and was a devoted husband and father.

One day, for insurance purposes, the couple took a saliva test. They were then asked to take a urine test. Finally they were asked to have a blood test. When they inquired why so many tests, they were told: 'We are checking on whether there are traces of HIV.' It was then that Peter confronted his wife and said, 'There is something that I haven't told you: there's another side to me that you don't know.'

Peter told her that before they got married he had lived a promiscuous life. He said that he had hoped marriage would put a stop to it, but that had not happened. He proceeded to tell his wife

of his many girlfriends during the years of their marriage. Mary nearly passed out. As she thought about the blood test, she screamed and wept.

The days of waiting seemed like months. Finally Mary got the results. She was fine – HIV negative. What a relief! Her husband got his results – HIV positive. Mary's world collapsed.

She had detected no clues, she had harboured no suspicions, she had received no warning. Her world was now in tatters. He had looked good to her; but when he came in through the door, he brought his baggage with him. Now the reality of Proverbs 14:12 (NKJV) became all too clear: 'There is a way which seems right to a man, but its end is the way of death.'

## Much care – but no prayer

Research conducted for one Christian denomination in the United States Pacific region indicated that seventeen per cent had gone through divorce after being baptized. Countless others can testify that they live a married life – 'all by myself'.

A minister confronted a dear lady in his church who was almost 82 years old. She had taught him years ago, and greatly inspired him. 'Sister McKinney,' he said, 'all these years you've been married, and your husband has never shared your faith. Yet I've never heard you complain. Tell me, how has it been for you?'

With a sigh that came from deep inside, she replied, 'Homer's taken very good care of me. He's given me all that I've asked for – all that I could want. A home, clothes, good food. Yes, he's taken good care of me.' Then with another shuddering sigh she went on: 'But no one can imagine the loneliness! There's no one in the morning to share my worship, no one to talk over the insights I obtain from Bible study. I go to church alone. No, no one can ever imagine the utter loneliness.'

## The Bible is for you too!

Many spouses who are not Christians are happy to remain with their Christian partners because they are treated well. There are biblical prescriptions that guide the Christian spouse's life:

To be spiritually lonely is to be lonely indeed.

| To the Christian man: | To the Christian woman: |
| --- | --- |
| 'If a Christian [man] has a wife who is not a Christian, but she wants to stay with him anyway, he must not leave her or divorce her. . . . For the unbelieving . . . wife is brought nearer to God by her Christian husband' (1 Corinthians 7:12-14).* | 'If a Christian woman has a husband who isn't a Christian, and he wants her to stay with him, she must not leave him. For the unbelieving husband is brought nearer to God by his Christian wife' (1 Corinthians 7:13, 14). |
| 'Love is very patient and kind, never jealous or envious, never boastful or proud, never haughty or selfish or rude. Love does not demand its own way. It is not irritable or touchy. It does not hold grudges and will hardly even notice when others do it wrong' (1 Corinthians 13:4, 5). | 'Wives, fit in with your husbands' plans; for then if they refuse to listen when you talk to them about the Lord, they will be won by your respectful, pure behaviour. Your godly lives will speak to them better than any words' (1 Peter 3:1). |
| 'If you love someone you will be loyal to him no matter what the cost. You will always believe in him, always expect the best of him, and always stand your ground in defending him' (1 Corinthians 13:7). | 'You wives, submit yourselves to your own husbands, for that is what the Lord has planned for you' (Colossians 3:18). |
| 'Husbands, show the same kind of love to your wives as Christ showed to the church when he died for her' (Ephesians 5:25). | 'You wives must submit to your husbands' leadership in the same way you submit to the Lord' (Ephesians 5:22). |
| 'You husbands must be loving and kind to your wives and not bitter against them, nor harsh' (Colossians 3:19). | 'So you wives must willingly obey your husbands in everything, just as the church obeys Christ' (Ephesians 5:24). |
| 'Drink from your own well, my son – be faithful and true to your wife' (Proverbs 5:15). | 'The wife must see to it that she deeply respects her husband – obeying, praising and honouring him' (Ephesians 5:33). |
| 'Rejoice in the wife of your youth. Let her charms and tender embrace satisfy you. Let her love alone fill you with delight. Why delight yourself with prostitutes, embracing what isn't yours? *For God is closely watching you*, and he weighs carefully everything you do' (Proverbs 5:18-21). | 'If you can find a truly good wife, she is worth more than precious gems! Her husband can trust her, and she will richly satisfy his needs. She will not hinder him, but help him all her life' (Proverbs 31:10-12). |

*All texts from New Living Translation.

## Struggle

The spiritually single fall into two categories: there are those who married, then one partner became a believer but the other did not share their faith. Then there are those who chose to marry someone who did not share their faith, believing that they would have more influence on the unbelieving partner than that partner would have on them. What a beautiful thought. They have discovered that life is a daily struggle, that absence of intimacy in the spiritual life is even more acute than absence of intimacy in the physical life.

Non-Christian spouses are often glad that you Christian spouses have all those rules, because they feel the rules will make you meek and gentle. Believe me, these non-Christian partners often know Bible texts – they know all that you should be doing and all that you shouldn't. What they don't realize is that the Bible is not just the rule book for Christians, every one of us is going to be judged by this book, whether we claim to believe it or not! Furthermore, James 4:17 says, 'Remember, too, that knowing what is right to do and then not doing it is sin.'

### Loneliness of the spiritually single

'There were times when it was acutely painful living a single Christian life – like when the doctor said I needed surgery and I could not go home and say, "Honey, pray with me." Other times, when I'd be reading a passage of scripture and some special truth would leap right off the page, without thinking, I'd turn to share it with him, only to be met by a frown, and the joy died on my lip, untold. I was married, but when it came to spiritual things, I was definitely single.'

Marcia Mitchell, *Spiritually Single.*

## 'It's only his drinking . . .' Really?

'After dating Bill for several months, Lila was head over heels in love and wanted to marry him. The only thing that bothered her was his drinking. He'd use any excuse: "I had a rough day at work!" "It's miserable outside." Despite her pastor's warnings, she went ahead and married him. Within two years it was a living hell. By now, he was drinking every night and becoming physically abusive. Heartbroken, Lila filed for divorce and they went their separate ways. Lila told her pastor, "I thought I knew what was best for me." She'd ignored all the warnings and made the biggest mistake of her life. *Any time a child of God marries a child of the devil, they're each going to have trouble with their father-in-law!* (Amos 3:3).'

Bob Gass, *The Word for Today.*

## Leaving your first love

Dear Dr Dobson,

I heard your radio programme today when you urged frustrated people not to get a divorce. It seemed like you were talking directly to me. But if I'm not going to get a divorce, then what can I do? Every day is worse than the one before and my husband and I are farther apart. I am more depressed than I've ever been.

My husband and I are thirty-four years old and we have four children. Chuck no longer cares about the things he used to love. He used to sing in the choir in church and work on a camper he was building for the family. Now he seems to be looking for a whole new way of life, spending his time dancing in bars and discos. He is involved with other women, spending money we can't afford, but nothing satisfies him for long. Tell me, what would you do if you were me?

My husband says I'm too old-fashioned, too moral. But I'm trying to live a Christian life. He says he would rather die than be a Christian. He makes me feel so dirty!

How do I continue this? I ask you. How?

Mabel

from Dr James Dobson, *Love Must Be Tough*

Satan is the enemy, not your partner.

## The real enemy

What we have to recognize in times of conflict is that 'we are not fighting against people made of flesh and blood, but against persons without bodies – the evil rulers of the unseen world, those mighty satanic beings and great evil princes of darkness who rule this world; and against huge numbers of wicked spirits in the spirit world' (Ephesians 6:12). It is not that your partner hates you, it's just that the devil in him/her hates the Holy Spirit in you. So pray. The devil cannot stand against the blood of Jesus, so claim it!

## No doormat

Now your non-believing spouse is making a big mistake if he or she thinks that being a Christian means being a doormat. As Dr James Dobson puts it, *love must be tough!* In fact there are some words (not concepts) which don't fit our modern vocabulary. While we know that *gay* means *happy,* nowadays we avoid using the word gay to describe a happy person. Similarly, while submission can be submission to the husband's love, not to his wishes, the word is so loaded today. There is nothing wrong with being gay when it means happy, and there is nothing wrong with being submissive when it means *mutual* submission, but the misunderstanding that surrounds the word has placed incredible burdens on a wife. The evil that has resulted from tossing this word submission around has been untold misery.

In her Bible commentary, *Patriarchs and Prophets,* page 59, Ellen White writes: 'Man's abuse of the supremacy thus given him has too often rendered the lot of woman very bitter and made her life a burden.' The Bible says our devotion must be to God and because we love Him so much, we love others so much. But let no one miss this point, *our love for our spouses, Christian or non-Christian, will not allow them to degrade our dignity, destroy our nobility and demolish our humanity.* I belong to Jesus before I belong to you!

## Love you or leave you?

One of the most difficult aspects of being spiritually single is believing you have what your spouse needs, but knowing you have to hold off until he seeks it for himself. This was Julia's dilemma.

'After my marriage,' she said, 'I quickly learned that I could not share my thoughts on spiritual matters with Jim. What he had politely listened to before we married suddenly made him prickly and defensive. Since we did not see eye to eye, he felt that I was infringing upon his personal views. He suspected that I had set out to change him. He was right, of course, in that each person must make his own decision for personal salvation. But when you truly love someone, can you stand by and let him drown?'

Let's look at things from your spouse's point of view.

Marriage changes things. Words that may have been politely tolerated in the days of courtship become bones of contention.

## What is your spouse going through?

It is likely that it is not just you who finds it difficult coping at home; your spouse probably does too. Here are some of the emotions that your spouse may be experiencing:

- Hurt
- Pressure
- Fear
- Being used
- Hostility
- Indifference
- Uneasiness
- Emotional separation
- Reticence
- Anger
- Resentment
- Jealousy

Now ask yourself the following questions:

* What ways can you think of to make your spouse more 'visible' in your church life? (Include him or her in church social activities, invite other Christian couples to your home for dinner, talk about your spouse as your unique helpmate, etc.).
* What would Christ's attitude be, regarding the balance between your church activities and your home life?
* In trying to view your church life from your spouse's point of view, what personal attitudes do you need to change in this situation?
* How can you lovingly ease the antag-

onism or threat that religion poses to your spouse regarding your children?

* If you have been clinging tightly to the 'right' to have a Christian husband, will you consider yielding this to Christ?

## Relating to your friends

Sometimes the loneliness is compounded because your spouse doesn't want to get too close to your friends. 'For eight or ten hours a week you don't share. For those hours you cannot possibly be company to one another,' says Lenore. 'And there's something more. The division causes a barrier with friends. For your spouse to show friendship would mean a commitment – one he's not ready to make.'

If your desire is to see God work in your partner's life, there are some things you can do to co-operate with the Holy Spirit.

## Put your spouse first

No, I'm not suggesting that you put him or her before your Lord, but I am saying that it is very easy to take your spouse for granted once you are married. Be actively involved in shaping the outcome of each day. Joyce Huggett suggests that when you wake up in the morning you should ask, 'How can I make my partner happy today?' It will bring your spouse to attention. It will make your partner take notice. It will cost you; but the rewards will be worth it.

Put your spouse first. Make him or her feel special. Do not take your partner for granted. A happy sustained relationship requires a degree of effort.

## Enjoy sex together

If it is true that in marriage the two become one, and if it is true that in marriage oneness means leaving, cleaving, and becoming one flesh, then sex is a vital part of marriage. *The fact that you are married to someone of a different faith, or even someone with no faith, does not change that!* In fact I would recommend that if the sexual side of your marriage is enjoyable and satisfying, it could have a rejuvenating effect on your whole relationship.

A couple came to see me, and the wife was in distress because her husband wanted to videotape their married sex to show friends. Thank God, not all spouses are like this! A good spouse will respect your sexual tastes. A good spouse will never want you to compromise your principles just to satisfy him. *The more a Christian wife can genuinely enjoy sex with her husband, the more he will feel loved, valued and appreciated.* It may cause him to reflect on the many positive qualities of his wife, and even her faith in God.

## Have fun together

Do those things that attracted you to each other in the first place – and then some! Dig out your old love-letters and read them aloud. Read over those cards you sent to each other. Play that board game that you haven't taken out for months, even years. Go out somewhere together.

Have fun together. Be adventurous together. Try new activities just for the fun of it.

Turn off the television for an hour *and enjoy each other's company* for a change. Try a new activity, just for a laugh.

**Just because you're a religious person doesn't mean you can't be a fun person.**

Paul Little, in his book *How to Give Away your Faith,* says that, as Christians, we should learn and remember five really funny clean jokes that we can share. How many can you say?

## Stay attractive

Don't let yourself go. You may not have the money of the Hollywood stars, but you are no less beautiful. Listen to the advice of close friends who want the best for you, with regard to your appearance. Don't just dress for yourself. Don't just eat to please yourself. Don't just wear the perfume or cologne that *you* like. Stay attractive *to* and *attracted* to your spouse.

## Prescriptive

As we have already stated, the Bible is both prescriptive and redemptive. Like a doctor, it prescribes what we should do if we want to remain healthy. It informs us of the dire consequences of

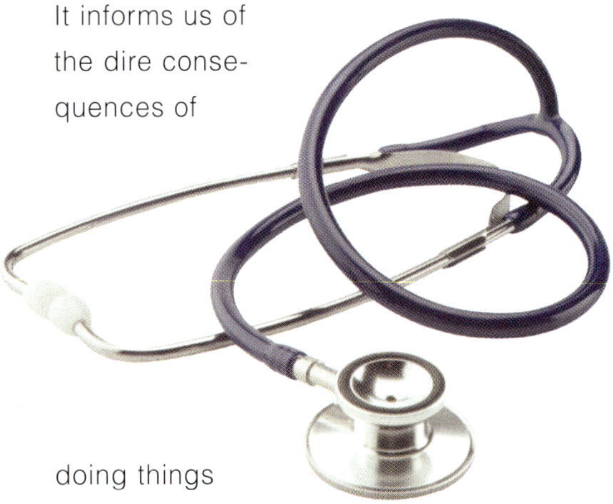

doing things our way, instead of God's way. It tells us that the God who made us knows what is best for us. It tells us, as Dr Dwight Nelson says, 'God is not a God to be afraid of. God is a God to be a friend of.' God's prescription can be summed up in the words, 'This do, and you shall live.'

So what should a person do to be preventative, to try to start out right? Watch, pray, consult and counsel. The Bible says, 'Where there is no counsel, the people fall: but in the multitude of counsellors there is safety' (Proverbs 11:14, NKJV).

An excellent questionnaire called PREPARE is available from Dr David Olson at the University of Minnesota. The following ten statements are used to discover spiritual compatibility:

- We share very similar spiritual beliefs.
- My partner and I feel closer because of our spiritual beliefs.
- We rely on our spiritual beliefs during difficult times.
- We are satisfied with how we express our spiritual values and beliefs.
- I believe our marriage must include active participation in church life.
- Spiritual differences cause some tension in our relationship.
- We have discussed the importance of our spiritual beliefs.
- My partner and I disagree about our spiritual beliefs.
- Sharing spiritual values helps our relationship grow.
- My spiritual beliefs are an important part of the commitment I have to my partner.

The *Spiritual Beliefs* series of statements are designed to assess attitudes, feelings and concerns about the meaning of religious beliefs and practices within the context of the relationship. Items focus on the meaning and importance of religion, involvement in church activities and the expected role that religious beliefs will have in the marriage.

A couple's satisfaction with their spiritual beliefs is not necessarily indicated by either a high or a low score but by the amount of agreement partners report. If both male and female scores are either high or low, they will tend to be satisfied with the role of religion in their relationship. If one partner is high and the other is low, a low degree of harmony is suggested, indicating that this area is potentially problematic.

## Redemptive

The Bible is also redemptive. It tells us that 'the wages of sin is death; but the free gift of God is eternal life through Jesus Christ our Lord' (Romans 6:23). It tells us that through Christ, winter will give way to spring, death will be followed by resurrection and defeat will be swallowed up in victory. If you are spiritually single, hold on to hope. ' "For there is hope for a tree – if it's cut down it sprouts again, and grows tender, new branches" ' (Job 14:7).

## Never alone

When we feel alone, we can take comfort in the reality that God will never leave us or forsake us. David said it this way, 'For if my father and mother should abandon me, you would welcome and comfort me' (Psalm 27:10).

We need to recognize that conversion is God's business. Sandra Finley Doran says in her book, *Every Time I Say Grace, We Fight:* 'To some, the issue of converting one's spouse is a lifelong battle, the stuff of which every argument is made. But the desire to convert one's spouse can actually spring from a number of motives, not all as pure as one might wish to believe.' One of these motives can be selfishness. Perhaps *your* life would be so much easier if only he or she were a fellow believer!

## Plan of action

If you are spiritually single, you need to discover ways of establishing open communication, nurturing individuality, managing conflict, fostering unconditional love, modelling acceptance. There are critical values of life, such as these, that instead of being modelled, can actually be destroyed, in the name of religion!

Do not let differences erase your love. Yearn for change, pray, fast even, but more important that even these is love. Paul says, 'Even if I had the gift of faith so that I could speak to a mountain and make it move, I would still be worth nothing at all without love' (1 Corinthians 13:2). I'm saying, you can have different beliefs as a married couple and still love each other! Remember those things that attracted you to your spouse, and while you are praying for your partner's spiritual life, *cherish those things!*

I think of Donna and Charmaine, two beautiful Christian women, both with wonderful husbands but whose partners do not share their faith. While it is clear that these women love their church and are the leaders of its youth programme, it is also abundantly clear that they love their husbands and are devoted to them. Through the dedication of these wives, their children have grown up to be committed to the Lord. Donna and Charmaine are not moping, moaning or morbid spouses, but hopeful, joyful and winsome. I believe God likes to work through loving people. I think that's why the apostle Paul said, 'Let love be your greatest aim' (1 Corinthians 14:1).

## Religion, resentment and rejection

'Shortly after our wedding I discovered that my husband and I held completely different viewpoints on the role that religion and church was to play in our lives. I was used to going to church every time the doors were open. At first my husband tolerated my religious schedule. But, as the years slipped by and he watched the physical and emotional drain on me as I spent time, energy and money on the church – when he thought I should be at home – then resentment set in. Any *good* I was doing for "others" was paralleled by the negative reaction of my husband. It was a whirlpool that dragged me constantly away from him. I was being sucked farther and farther away from him until our worlds rarely touched and I wondered at times why we even stayed married.'

Marcia Mitchell, *Spiritually Single.*

## It's a piece of cake

Dr Kembleton Wiggins, from Barbados, tells the story of a woman who spoke to him about her passionate desire for her husband to share her faith. 'I've tried everything, pastor,' she wailed. 'What exactly have you tried?' asked Pastor Wiggins. 'I've stopped cooking his food. I've even stopped sleeping in bed with him at nights!' Dr Wiggins replied, 'No wonder the man won't join your church!' He asked her if she would be prepared to do it his way, whereupon she replied that as she had tried everything else, she had nothing to lose.

'What is his favourite food?' asked Dr Wiggins.

'Cake,' she replied unequivocally.

'Now you go home and bake him the best cake you've ever baked,' said Wiggins. 'Bring him his slippers. Run your fingers through his hair, and say to him, "I love you." '

The woman said, 'Pastor, if I should ever do that, the poor man would faint.'

'Faint or no faint,' continued Dr Wiggins, 'just do it!'

Later on in Dr Wiggins' series of meetings, the lady came to a meeting with a handsome gentleman on her arm, and when the call was made to give their lives to Jesus, the husband came forward in surrender. 'What all the chiding and complaining didn't do,' says Dr Wiggins, 'a little cake and "I love you" did.'

I know we all wish it could be so easy, but the two strategies you must follow can be summed up in this: Pray as if everything depended upon God and then work as if everything depended on you.

A man used to brag to his friends in the bar, 'No matter what time I come home at night, my wife will get up and fix me something to eat.' Some didn't believe. Others enquired, 'Why does she do this?' 'I don't know why she does it, exactly,' the man replied, 'but it's something to do with the church she goes to.'

His friends wanted to see it for themselves. So at 3am they arrived at the man's house. True to form, his wife descended the stairs, greeted the guests, went into the kitchen, fixed five plates of food, and then retired to bed. The friends were amazed. They said, 'We've seen it now, with our own eyes.' They ate and left. Like the prodigal son, the man came to his senses. He asked himself, 'Why *does* she do it? I will go and find out.'

He went upstairs and shook his wife. 'Honey, honey,' he said, 'no matter what time I come home you get up and fix me something to eat. Why do you do it?'

'Well,' she replied, 'I figure that being as you're going to miss out on heaven . . . I'd just give you a little heaven down here!'

True story! That man is now a deacon in his wife's church. Let's keep believing it. The unbelieving spouse can be won over by the caring concern of a compassionate, Christian spouse!

# Solowork on Chapter 5

## Thriving, striving, and surviving

It is your words and His Word that will see you through. The Bible says, 'They overcame him by the blood of the Lamb, and by the word of their testimony' (Revelation 12:11, KJV). Take some time and fill in the spaces below.

| Where I was | Where I am | Where I want to be |
| --- | --- | --- |
| | | |

| What's stopping me | How I can overcome |
| --- | --- |
| | |

## READ ON!

| Author | Book title | Publisher |
| --- | --- | --- |
| Branner, Esmie | Beyond the Veil of Darkness | Pacific Press |
| Doran, Sandra Finley | Every Time I Say Grace, We Fight | Review & Herald |
| Mitchell, Marcia L | Spiritually Single | Bethany House |

# Chapter 6

# After the love has gone

Dear Pastor Brown

It is not without great sadness that I write this letter. I also write with desperation. Ten years ago you conducted the wedding of Joanne and myself. I know I have not kept in touch with you as much as I should but things have changed so rapidly and dramatically.

When Joanne and I got married, things looked good. But when you saw us last at my brother's wedding, our marriage was undoubtedly on the rocks. I could tell that you perceived as much, but I was ashamed to admit anything to anyone.

Joanne and I are now separated and although I still love her, I can see no way of reconciliation. All attempts on my behalf have been taken by Joanne as hostility. I feel there has been no attempt on her side. And now I may have made things harder for any reconciliation.

I know Joanne has faith in very few people. I also know that very few of those in whom she trusts have your understanding of marriage in general and her in particular. It's possible that because I am part of the problem, I am blinded by my own wants and needs. With this in mind I ask for your help.

You are our last hope. Please, please HELP!

Philip

## End of family life

The front-page headline of the *Daily Mail,* 23 August 1995, read 'End of Family Life in Britain: Scandal of teenage mothers as divorces hit a record level.'

The article went on to say, 'The collapse of marriage and family life in Britain was laid bare yesterday. The extent of the crisis emerged as a Government census report showed divorce at record levels.'

The following year a Sunday newspaper headline read as follows: 'Pregnant at 15, Married at 16, Divorced at 17.' The story read: 'Gymslip mum Clare Edge is facing up to life as a divorcee – at the tender age of 17. She was pregnant at 15 and married at 16. Now, with her dream marriage in tatters, the devastated youngster has experienced more than many women twice her age. As her pals agonize over exam results and fashions, Clare struggles with court papers, solicitors and child support

### *It's a different world today*

| | 1850 | 1900 | 1950 | 2000 |
|---|---|---|---|---|
| SOCIETY | Agrarian | Industrial | Information | Global |
| ECONOMY | Agricultural | Manufacturing | Service | High-Tech |
| WORK TIME | Nature | Clock | Flexitime | Relative |
| TRADE CENTRE | Mediterranean | Atlantic | Pacific | Trilateral |
| FORM | Tribe | Town | Technopolis | Neo-Village |
| TRAVEL | Walking | Driving | Flying | Teleporting |
| WORLDVIEW | Familial | National | Global | Ecological |
| ORIENTATION | Past | Present | Future | Future-Past |
| ETHNIC VIEW | Conformity | University | Diversity | Mutuality |
| POWER/SOURCE | Family/Muscle | State/Money | Individual/Mind | Networks/Empowerment |
| EDUCATION | Grade School | High School | College/Grad | Grad-Tech/Cyber U |
| LEARNING | Kinesthetic | Auditory | Visual | Triadic |
| LOYALTY | Family | Institution | Individual | Group |
| OPTIONS | Minimal | Many | Multiple | Myriad |
| LIFESTYLE | Ritual | Reformation | Revolution | Reliance |
| RELIGION | Tribal | Organized | Self-Help | Spirituality |
| VIEW OF GOD | Mythical | Ontological | Functional | Inclusive |

adapted from Caleb Rosado, *Stages of Societal Change.*

for her daughter Natasha, now 20 months old. And the pretty brunette admits sadly: "If Natasha finds herself in the same position as a teenager, I'll definitely tell her, 'Please don't do it.'" '

How do you bounce back?

## It happens

I saw the following seminars advertised in a Toronto brochure: 'Help! Coping With the Crisis of Separation'; 'Surviving the Break Up' and 'The Impact of Separation and Divorce on Children'.

They offered 'Rainbows: peer support groups for children who have experienced death, divorce or other painful transition in their family.' When I saw all these programmes about divorce, all I could conclude was – it happens. That's the reality of life today. We are a global village caught up with the excitement of a technological future and ignoring the stability of a traditional past.

## Emergency – fire, fire!

In Oklahoma – among the top five states in frequency of divorce, with 6 per 1000 in 1998 – Governor Frank Keating is urging ministers, lawyers, psychologists and others to mount a campaign to reduce the divorce rate by a third within ten years. In Arkansas, also in the top five with 6.1 per

Children are the real victims of divorce – but recieve scant attention when the decision to divorce is arrived at.

Marriages need to be born-again – on a regular basis. The born-again marriage can be a fun-filled experience.

1000, the governor has declared a 'marital emergency' and is seeking to halve the divorce rate in the next ten years.

## The fire engine?

While marriage *preparation* is important, marriage *maintenance* is vital. One commonly untapped resource is the mentoring available from the army of healthy marriages in our community. Mick McManus has organized a very successful programme entitled *Marriage Savers* (www.marriagesavers.org) whose philosophy states: 'Every congregation has couples with solid marriages who really could be of help to other couples, but have never been asked, inspired or trained to come alongside another couple at a key stage of their life.'

When the programme ran in two counties of Kansas City, divorce rates plummeted by 35 per cent in just two years. But what about when it all breaks down? Is there life after divorce – after the love has gone?

## Acceptance

The question many are asking today is, *Why has divorce skyrocketed so much?*

There are at least five reasons.

* Firstly, *acceptance.* There is today a general acceptance of divorce. People marry with divorce as the safety net. Like abortion, the scars are not realized until

after the event. Couples do not understand that divorce is not the only option for a broken marriage, neither is it the first option. Couples accept divorce because, like Humpty Dumpty, they have fallen off their wall, and they are convinced that all the king's horses and all the king's men cannot put Humpty together again.

* The second reason why divorce has skyrocketed is *individualism.* The doctrine of individualism is gripping the world like an ice cold artic wind – and the wind is blowing from the west. Naphtal Rucibwa, professor of Public Health in Rwanda, identifies three strengths of families in Africa:

**1)** Strong belief that in marriage two people become one without the will of either being submerged into that of the other; **2)** family loyalty not seen in the West; and **3)** belief that marriage is not an affair of two individuals, but the affair of families. Thus divorce, while being a problem of the couple, is largely a problem of families, consequently families attempt to resolve the conflict.

* The third reason for the divorce statistics going through the roof is *affluence.* Traditionally the family was a self-sufficient productive unit. Survival was difficult outside the family. Not any more. Economic independence has provided the fuel that drives the divorce train. But the words of Dr Benjamin Carson are still true. He says: 'Delayed gratification is a valid entity. You don't have to have everything right away.'

'The doctrine of individualism is gripping the world like an ice-cold arctic wind – and the wind is blowing from the West.'

## 7 telltale signs that your marriage is in trouble

* You no longer talk to each other.
* You no longer hold hands, kiss or caress.
* Your sex life is boring.
* Every discussion or disagreement escalates into a major fight.
* You take your mate for granted and no longer take the time to look attractive.
* You let other people (relatives/children) and things (job) come between you.
* You don't do things together any more.

* The fourth reason is social disruption arising from *war*. It is impossible to overstate the effect of the two world wars on our society. Until then, divorce levels were fairly stable. People abandoned caution and propriety when they were separated from their partners. People had a quick marriage or a quick affair 'for the sake of the country'. The two world wars introduced great uncertainty into people's thinking which led to a change in the divorce laws. Canada's Divorce Act was introduced in 1968. It became easy to get into marriage and easy to get out.

* The final reason for the soaring divorce rate is simply *the secularization of life*. Jonathan Sachs, Chief Rabbi in Britain, said in a Reith Lecture: 'Removing the legal and moral sting from cohabitation, divorce, illegitimacy and homosexuality does not leave the world unchanged. The gradual transformation by which sin becomes immorality, immorality becomes deviance, deviance becomes choice, and all choice becomes legitimate, is a profound redrawing of our moral landscape.'

Martin Henry wrote in the *Jamaica Gleaner*, 20 January 2000: 'Divorce rates are rising everywhere. The family is rooted in religion. The attempt to build a great civilization on purely secular foundations which the humanism of the Enlightenment prescribes is unprecedented in history.' But how does global divorce affect the individual?

## Emotional divorce

The first visible sign of a deteriorating marriage is likely to be what psychiatrists call 'emotional divorce'. This is when one or both partners withhold emotion from their relationship because they have become uncertain of how they feel towards their spouse. They may still go to social functions together, still attend church together, *but the fire has gone out.* The attraction has gone. The trust has gone.

It is natural and healthy for couples, as time goes on, to grow in different areas.

Healthy marriages will establish bonds of interdependence. There is no desire for dependence of any kind in emotional divorce, just antagonism and disappointment.

## How can you survive divorce?

***Emergency treatment***

* Believe you have value.
* Pray.
* Have a biblical optimism.
* Enlist friends.
* Minimize painful memories.
* Watch for excessive stress.
* Have an exercise programme.
* Practise problem ownership.
* Read.

***Long-term care***

* Increase confidence.
* Make choices.
* Make commitments.
* Set short-term & long-term goals.
* Trust in God.

## Legal divorce

In most societies we have turned over to the courts the responsibility for formalizing the dissolution of marriages. While some people have tried to make a celebration out of their divorce, it is a tragedy, even when it is a blessing. A death, as it were, has taken place. Often the stages of grief: pain, shock, blame, denial, guilt and anger will be felt just as much as in the death of a loved one. It may take a long time before there is a resolution to the turmoil.

## Economic divorce

In many societies husband and wife are regarded as an economic unit. When a household is broken up by divorce, economic settlement must be made. Many times the settlement of property and assets is so acrimonious that if there had been any spark of hope that the marriage could be salvaged, it has now been extinguished.

## Community divorce

When a couple divorce, their community is automatically affected. Friends' relationships to the couple are changed. People take sides. There is disapproval. There is ostracism. For many divorcing people, the divorce from the community may make it seem that nothing in the world is stable.

## Psychic divorce

Finally comes divorce of the mind. It is the process of becoming autonomous as an individual, rather than as a couple. Psychic divorce is almost always last, and always the most difficult. The length of time during which a person involved in a divorce suffers intense pain varies with the individual. Three to nine months is common. A second phase follows that generally lasts between six and twelve months. For many, it usually takes between two and four *years* of processing the emotions after the divorce is finalized before they are ready to marry again.

## Remarriage

If the divorce was on biblical grounds then the remarriage is, too! For many, the thought of remarriage fills them with fear and trepidation. Will my next marriage experience the trauma of divorce or death? Many have to cope not only with their own fears, but also the fears of their friends. Remarriage must be contemplated on the following platform:

* *Reconciliation* – The guilty are to reconcile or remain single. Then we must all reconcile with God (1 Corinthians 7:10, 11; 2 Corinthians 5:18, 19).
* *Remorse* – God hates divorce and cruel men. Speak tenderly again. Try to transform your Valley of Troubles into a Door of Hope (Malachi 2:15, 16; Hosea 2:14, 15).
* *Reconstruction* – Though devastated, a godly person can rise again and live once more in peace and harmony (Proverbs 24:16; 1 Corinthians 7:15).

Unlike divorce, little attention has been devoted to the high rate of remarriage after divorce. The problems associated with remarital adjustment are often heightened by the fact that partners in remarriage may still be adjusting to their divorces. An individual can be struggling to establish bonds of affection, commitment and trust with their new partner, while still dealing with emotional ties to their former spouse.

Before remarriage can work successfully emotional baggage from any previous relationship has to be sorted out.

## The friendship game – round 2

Typically the remarriage process begins with the emotional remarriage. This is the often slow process by which a divorced person re-establishes a bond of attraction, commitment and trust with a member of the opposite sex.

Then there is the mental and actual process of changing from being an individual to being a couple. Somebody else is around now, in your stuff! It can be exciting – it can also be scary. Not as scary, though, as when you have to 'go

## Forming a new friendship

**Do**

* Act your age (in dress, manner of speech, etc.).
* Solicit input from your children.
* Be honest about:
  your previous marriage
  your past accomplishments
  your children
  your goals for the relationship.
* Be conscious of the example you are setting for your children.

**Don't**

* Say 'I'll call you' if you really don't intend to continue the relationship.
* Insist on taking your friend to places where she/he is uncomfortable.
* Assume roles with your partner's children to which you are not entitled.

Ray and Jennifer Minner, adapted

## The Stepfamily Cycle

*A child's perspective*

'I really hope my parents will get back together' – ***fantasy***

'I'm glad you're here, but don't come in!' – ***awkwardness***

'Leave me to work this out' – ***awareness***

'Let's get some things clear' – ***mobilization***

'What can we do together?' – ***action***

'You're not so bad after all' – **intimacy**

'We're going to make it' – ***resolution***

public'. Some like it; so don't. Some will grow to accept it; some won't. Some friends you will gain; some you will lose. That's just the way it is.

It's one thing when the hard time comes from your friends; you can take that. But it's quite another thing when it comes from your children. One stepmother put it this way: 'I was trying so hard to make these two broken pieces of plate go together. But they were from different plates and they just didn't fit!' When a couple divorces, a 'double single-parent' stage begins in which children become part of two single-parent families.

## How to tell the children

Let me share seven suggestions on informing your children that your marriage has come to an end:

**1)** Decide in advance how you are going to explain it to the children and ensure that both of you are present. Don't let them hear two different versions.

**2)** Be as frank as is reasonably possible. Don't try to bluff them by giving them implausible scenarios, or by suggesting that the separation is temporary when you know it is not.

**3)** Assure them that they are loved as much as ever and that it is in no way their fault.

**4)** Emphasize the things that will *not* change in their lives. Children are conservative and find the thought of upheaval stressful.

**5)** It is not necessary to pretend to be best friends with your spouse when you are not. But try at least to be cordial to each other in the presence of the children.

**6)** Work hard at making arrangements for visits and handovers in advance. Don't humiliate your children.

**7)** Don't despair. Use the opportunity to

improve the relationship with your children.

## Guilt

When the love is gone, there is one thing that often remains: guilt. How do you handle it?

* Ask God to bring to your mind the things you feel guilty about and write them down;
* Divide your guilt into two categories: justified and unnecessary;
* Mark those items where you know you have really done something wrong;
* Ask God to forgive you for each wrong;
* Begin to seek the forgiveness of each wronged individual;
* Don't phone or write those whom it might embarrass or trouble.

Be careful with the letters you write. Some people's letters are like poison. I have made it a rule never to write negative letters. They are too permanent. William Barclay, in his autobiography *Testament of Faith,* tells how he had something against his headmaster and wrote a particularly strong letter to him. The headmaster called him in and said to him, 'I can understand why you wrote this letter, son – but why did you post it?' If there are things you need to get out of your system, do so. Write them down, cry over them if necessary, then screw the paper up and throw it away. Only mail your regret over the part *you* played. Your guilt may only be a part of the problem – but it's the only part you have control over.

## From chaos to comfort

While we may live in several time zones, we all live in the same life zones. There is the chaotic zone, which we generally find too risky. Then there is the stretch zone which is risky, but manageable. Finally, there is the comfort zone – the zone with no risks at all.

Life events and life transitions pitch us into the chaotic zone and then quickly back into the rigid boundaries of the comfort zone. The task of counselling is to enable us to manage the process of extending the comfort zone further. In so doing, we will feel a resistance to the challenge of change. Life is about new learning, fresh negotiation, adaptation and

## Twenty ways to save (or improve) your marriage

* Make the effort to share a special meal or some other treat together.
* Take a hot bath together.
* Write love letters to each other.
* Watch the sunrise together and give thanks for each other.
* Listen to your partner. Pay close attention to what he or she is saying and not saying.
* Surround yourself with Christian married couples who also support your marriage.
* Make time for your partner. Work to making him or her your best friend.
* Bring your best home. Many people share more with their colleagues than they do with their mate. Don't commit emotional adultery.
* Tell the truth.
* Do the right thing. When faced with choices, choose the one that will strengthen the marriage.
* Share your feelings.
* Give your partner a surprise gift.
* Look at your wedding album.
* Revisit the place of your first date.
* Re-energize your sex life.
* Determine to resolve conflict. Make a list of issues affecting your relationship and regularly sit down together to address them.
* Accept your partner's temperament (extrovert, introvert) and praise the strengths.
* Remember your marriage vows, 'For better *or for worse*'. Don't let unrealistic expectations ruin your marriage.
* Cast all your burdens on God, because He cares for you.
* Visit a marriage counsellor when times get tough.

Adapted from *Ebony*

## Making your relationship work

First: it is not too late. If you do not allow yourself to believe and accept that, you will think your way out of this relationship before we have had a chance to save it. You may think your relationship has failed, you may feel like you have tried everything, you may feel tired, deflated, and defeated, but I'm telling you, you have to get that thought out of your head or you're dead in the water with an anvil tied around your ankle. No matter how many times you've been hurt – no matter how many times you've been disappointed, no matter how many times you've believed it could be different only to get slapped in the face again – you have to be willing to give yourself one more chance.

Dr Phillip McGraw, *Relationship Rescue.*

accommodation to ✸ new constructs (at a cognitive level); ✸ new behaviours (at a behavioural level); and ✸ new awareness (at a feeling level). To a large extent, life is not predictable, it's not about black or white, it's about living life in the grey. Ultimately, we must have a greater tolerance for ambiguity.

## Better off?

Judith Wallerstein made a study of couples who divorce and discovered that a quarter of them suffer from loneliness and depression, sixty per cent of second marriages end in divorce, and only ten per cent say they have happier, fuller lives ten years after their divorce. Thank God, if

you have remarried, you can be among the ten per cent!

That's why Larry Richards entitled his book *Remarriage: A Healing Gift from God.* For you, weeping has endured for a night; joy can come to you now. Yesterday was the mourning; today is the morning. *Can your marriage be saved?* You can either work actively to salvage the relationship or you can look the reality of divorce straight in the eye – and deny it!

## Did we make a mistake?

We were invited to their wedding. The night before the wedding it finally hit her. She was making a terrible mistake! He didn't want to meet her friends. He just about tolerated her family. He was into his friends – and himself. They got married, had a child – and they divorced. Before marriage, pray four times a day. It's never too late to get out – no matter how much money you've spent on wedding plans. After marriage, though, never entertain the idea that your marriage was a mistake.

If you wonder whether it's worth all the effott trying to save your marriage, let me answer you. It is. Whatever you think the end results of your efforts may be, start the engine – you're in for a long ride.

## The long road back

* *Begin at the beginning.* Go back to that vow you made. Bob Moeller says in his book *For Better, For Worse, For Keeps,* 'The way to renew a marriage doesn't begin with a change of emotions, but with an act of will.' Agree that divorce will not be an option and take it from there.
* *Let go of past hurts.* Acknowledge where you've each gone wrong, ask for forgiveness, and then say, 'Forgetting the past and looking forward to what lies ahead, I strain to reach the end of the race . . . .' (Philippians 3:13, 14).
* *Keep going until you get there.* As somebody said, the only way out is through.
* *Dare to believe.* Believe, even if only one person seems committed to the relationship. I like how Claudia Arp puts it: 'God needs only one heart to begin to work in a relationship.'
* *Give it time.* One person said, 'Did we make a mistake? It doesn't matter any more. What matters is the love we've found from the God who redeems and makes all things new.'

# Solowork on Chapter 6

## Making counselling work for you

Many who have encountered divorce have also encountered some form of counselling at one time or another. Take some time right now and review lessons from the past and strategies for the future.

### *Experience of counselling*

**Came with . . .** ............................................................

**Went through . . .** ............................................................

**Discovered . . .** ............................................................

**Left with . . .** ............................................................

### *When you hit a bad patch*

**FIRST AID . . .** ............................................................

***Don't wait until a problem is overwhelming***

**READ ON!**

| Author | Book title | Publisher |
|---|---|---|
| Warnke, Mike & Warnke, Rose Hall | Recovering from Divorce: There is Hope & Healing for Victims | Victory House |
| Smoke, Jim | Suddenly Single | Fleming H. Revell |
| Wimberly, Edward P. | Counselling African American Marriages and Families | John Knox Press |

# Chapter 7

# Only for the children

## Surviving as a single parent

I am a single parent. There are many of us who sit beside you in the pews each week at church. Each of us has arrived at this place by our own private road, well marked with tears and heartbreak.

If our singleness is the result of a death or divorce, we and our children have suffered a massive psychological wallop.

Without question, however, the heaviest psychological toll falls on the children themselves. Their familiar and dependable world is suddenly cleaved apart. They are thrown upon a parent who must play both father and mother to them. There are times when we long to go 'off-duty' for a while – but we can't, because a recognized given of single parenting is that our children's need for extra care and reassurance is inversely proportional to the amount of energy we have at any given moment.

There's no denying that a broken home presents one of life's greatest challenges to a single parent's time, resources and energy. There are no pat answers or short-cuts. Each step of progress comes at the cost of great pain.

It's important to know that many children raised in single parent homes become mature, responsible, happy adults, testimony that the quality of parenting, not the 'quantity' of parents, counts most in raising children.

Jeannette Johnson

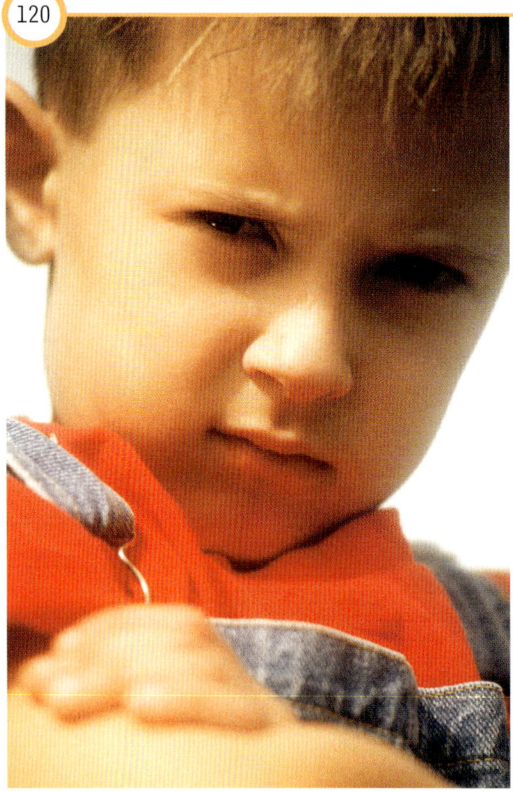

## Hurting children

Some years ago a song came out that said, 'Only for the children, I keep love alive. Only for the children, my love survives.' That's what keeps many single parents going – their love for their children.

Of his 385 pupils, 75 per cent no longer live with both their parents, says a head-master in Coventry, England. A head-mistress in Exeter reports that she once had a class of 22 where not one child was living with both its natural parents. Some changed their name several times while they were in school. Staff had to be extremely careful how they spoke about marriage and the family lest they convey to the children that they came from relationships which were not acceptable. In some schools, teachers no longer talk about parents, but of the 'special people' the children live with.

## Hurting parents

The 1992 and 1994 United States Census Bureau Reports told us that there were more than 3,349,000 divorced single mothers and more than 664,000 divorced single fathers in America. Many would be happy; many would be hurting. This book was written for them. Single mothers and bachelor fathers abound – so do their children. More than 16,334,000 children under the age of eighteen are living in a home with a mother only, and more than 2,257,000 children under eighteen live with a father only.

In 1901 there were 477 divorces in Britain. In 1941 there were 6,400. In 1993 there were 165,000. Now the new century records over 200,000 divorces. What are the valleys in single parenting? Are there any mountains? Let single parents tell their own story.

## A single mother's story

A single-parent student of mine, Merissa, interviewed Cynthia, a single parent in full-time study, with one son, Ryan (all names are changed):

*Merissa:* 'Tell me some of the negative elements you find in single parenting.'

*Cynthia:* 'Sole responsibility. Exhaustion, physically and emotionally. Having to play both roles. Having to play football when I don't feel like it – rough play, because boys love rough play. Explaining why mum and dad are not together. Also knowing that even with my best efforts, I can't successfully play a mother and father role. Feeling the emotions he's feeling, knowing that he really wants both parents together, and that he's denied that.'

*Merissa:* 'Tell me some of the pros of being a single parent.'

*Cynthia:* 'I don't need to consult my husband. Ryan and I discuss things. We're best friends. We share secrets. There's a strong bond. He sees himself as the man of the house. He says, "Mummy, I'll look after you." We also treasure our space. There's a time when he wants to be alone, and he says, "Mummy, I want to be on my own." And I do the same.'

*Merissa:* 'What hopes do you have for him?'

*Cynthia:* 'Oh, I have great hopes for him. He's reading *Think Big* by Dr Ben Carson, at the moment. He's self-motivated after reading that. He's very mature, respectful and appreciative. And spiritually, it's great. We have our quiet times. Me, Ryan and God. It's as if God is acting as Father . . . . '

*Merissa:* 'How does Ryan feel as a person?'

*Cynthia:* 'There are times when he will say, "I wish daddy were here. I want

mummy to marry my dad." I think that deep inside he knows that something is missing. Somewhere inside he's wishing his father was around.'

## Go for the gusto

Interviews such as this one, along with the testimonies of our own family members, have given my wife and I a window into

# Mothers

A few months ago, when I was picking up the children at school, another mother I knew well rushed up to me. Emily was fuming with indignation. 'Do you know what you and I are?' she demanded. Before I could answer, and I didn't really have one handy – she blurted out the reason for her question. It seemed she had just returned from renewing her driver's license at the County Clerk's office. Asked by the woman recorder to state her 'occupation', Emily had hesitated, uncertain how to classify herself. 'What I mean is,' explained the recorder, 'Do you have a job, or are you just a . . . ?'

'Of course I have a job,' snapped Emily. 'I'm a mother.'

'We don't list "mother" as an occupation . . . "housewife" covers it,' said the recorder emphatically.

I forgot all about her story until one day I found myself in the same situation, this time at our own Town Hall. The clerk was obviously a career woman, poised, efficient, and possessed of a high-sounding title, like 'Official Interrogator' or 'Town Registrar.'

'And what is your occupation?' she probed. What made me say it, I do not know. The words simply popped out:

'I'm . . . a Research Associate in the Field of Child Development and Human Relations.' The clerk paused, ball-point pen frozen in midair, and looked up as though she had not heard right. I repeated the title slowly, emphasizing the most significant words. Then I stared with wonder as my pompous pronouncement was written in bold, black ink on the official questionnaire.

both the pain and promise of single parenting, and have often left us staggering in admiration and wonder at the will not just to survive, but to thrive.

I think of Lydia Davis Barrett, interviewed in *Ebony* magazine. Lydia, 47, is president of the Urban League of Essex County, New Jersey. A former welfare caseworker, she found herself receiving welfare shortly after her husband, she says, 'left a note on my pillow' and walked out eighteen years ago. After two years on welfare she landed a job as a secretary and began formulating a plan for her life.

Her children received university scholarships and she eventually earned a Master's degree in public administration. She says, 'As single mothers, we don't

'Might I ask,' said the clerk with new interest, 'just what you do in your field?' Coolly, without any trace of fluster in my voice, I heard myself reply:

'I have a continuing programme of research (what mother doesn't?) in the laboratory and in the field (normally I would have said indoors and out). I'm working for my Masters (the whole darned family) and already have four credits (all daughters). Of course, the job is one of the most demanding in the humanities (any mother care to disagree?) and I often work fourteen hours a day (twenty-four is more like it). But the job is more challenging than most run-of-the-mill careers and the rewards are in satisfaction rather than just money.'

There was an increasing note of respect in the clerk's voice as she completed the form, stood up, and personally ushered me to the door. As I drove into our driveway buoyed up by my glamorous new career, I was greeted by my lab assistants – aged 13, 7, and 3. And, upstairs, I could hear our new experimental model (six months) in the child-development programme, testing out a new vocal pattern.

I felt triumphant. I had scored a beat on bureaucracy. And I had gone down on the official records as someone more distinguished and indispensable to mankind than 'just another . . . .' Home . . . what a glorious career. Especially when there's a title on the door.

'A mother and proud.'

have to settle for the minimum that society has to offer. We can go for the gusto!'

## What would you pay a mother for her work?

Insurance firm United Friendly looked at the average mum's day to help it calculate how much cover would be needed to protect the family if she became ill or had an accident. They calculated that the average mother does nine jobs: child-minder, cook, driver, housecleaner, laundry-worker, finance clerk, decorator, teacher and nurse. The insurance firm concluded that it would cost £41,000 (US$63,000) a year to hire someone to do all the chores she was doing for nothing.

No wonder Bishop T. D. Jakes said in his book, *Help! I'm Raising My Children Alone:* 'Recently our insurance agent increased the death benefit on my wife's policies. It was not because she is the primary breadwinner. It was because she contributes things to the children and myself that would be difficult if not impossible to replace. They are not just monetary; they are in other arenas. His reason for increasing the policy was simple. If I had to hire someone to provide what she gives to the family, it would be expensive and, to a degree, impossible.'

## Never enough time!

When Jeanette Johnson, editor of *Guide* (a magazine for teenagers), was a small girl her mother told her, 'Don't waste my time crying. There's good to be had from every situation. Look for it!' After

# How much time do you have?

The man came home from work late again, tired and irritated to find his 5-year-old son waiting for him at the door.

'Daddy, may I ask you a question?'

'Yeah, sure, what is it?' replied the man.

'Daddy, how much money do you make an hour?'

'That's none of your business! What makes you ask such a thing?' the man said angrily.

'I just want to know. Please tell me, how much do you make an hour?' pleaded the little boy.

'If you must know, I make $20 an hour.'

'Oh,' the little boy replied, head bowed. Looking up, he said, 'Daddy, may I borrow $10, please?'

The father was furious. 'If the only reason you wanted to know how much money I make is just so you can borrow some to buy a silly toy or some other nonsense, then you march yourself straight to your room and go to bed. Think about why you're being so selfish. I work long, hard hours every day and don't have time for such childish games.'

The little boy quietly went to his room and shut the door. The man sat down and started to get even madder about the little boy's questioning. How dare he ask such questions only to get some money? After an hour or so, the man had calmed down, and started to think he may have been a little hard on his son. Maybe there was something he really needed to buy with that $10, and he didn't ask for money very often. The man went to the little boy's room and opened the door.

'Are you asleep, son?' he asked.

'No, Daddy, I'm awake,' replied the boy.

'I've been thinking, maybe I was too hard on you earlier,' said the man. 'It's been a long day and I took my aggravation out on you. Here's that $10 you asked for.'

The little boy sat straight up, beaming. 'Oh, thank you Daddy!' he yelled. Then, reaching under his pillow, he pulled out some more crumpled-up bills. The man, since the boy already had money, started to get angry again.

The little boy slowly counted out his money, then looked up at his father.

'Why did you want more money if you already had some?' the father grumbled.

'Because I didn't have enough, but now I do,' the little boy replied. 'Daddy, I have $20. Can I buy an hour of your time?'

Jeanette's divorce she thought about her mother's advice, while managing three jobs and three children. Recognizing that she seemed to have too little time, too little money, and too little energy, she decided to make up the following rules of her own:

* ***Don't brood over your change of fortunes.*** If you're going to survive, you don't have time to rehearse all the events that brought you to where you are today. As T. D. Jakes says, 'Use the past to fertilize the future.'
* ***Set aside a specific time each day for your child that is his or hers to control.*** Susannah Wesley had planned time for each of her children – and she had 19!
* ***Establish and maintain a daily routine.*** One of the most healing things we can do for our children is to make life predictable again. That will mean working to be accessible to our children in their moments of excitement or pain.

Somebody said, 'Yesterday is a cancelled cheque. Tomorrow is a promissory note. Today is the only cash you have. So spend it wisely.'

## Never enough money!

A boy wrote to his father: 'No mon, no fun, your son.' His father wrote back: 'So sad, too bad, your dad.' Humorous perhaps, but the reality is that for most single parents money is in short supply, there is too much month left at the end of the money. Therefore,

* ***Make a budget and stick to it!*** This doesn't increase the take-home pay, but it makes a difference in how far it goes. The Bible says, 'Let each one of you [personally] put aside something and save it up as he has prospered [in proportion to what he is given]' (1 Corinthians 16:2, Amplified Bible). Put some money aside for God, and put some in saving for yourself.
* ***Include your children as partners in this budget-balancing act.*** Don't expect them to become a substitute for a former marriage partner, but give them a more-than-average say. Teach them the meaning of expenses versus income, and teach them to put their trust in God. The Bible says, 'Don't worry at all about having enough food and clothing. Why be like the heathen? For they take pride in all these things and are deeply concerned about them. Your heavenly Father already knows perfectly well that you need them, and he will gladly give them to you if you give him first place in your life' (Matthew 6:31 33).
* ***Put God first.*** You will be surprised to see how far your money will stretch when you put God first. A twenty-dollar note was having a conversation with a one-dollar note. Where have you been, lately?' asked the one dollar note. The twenty-dollar responded, 'I've been to the horse races, the theatre, the football games, the movies, the finest restaurants, oh, I've been having a good time, what about you? Where have you been?' The one-dollar note replied, 'Oh, the usual place. Church, church, church.' Put God first. 'If you do, I will open up the windows of heaven for you and pour out a blessing so great you won't have room enough to take it in!' (Malachi 3:10).

## Understanding lone parents

A parent without a partner is faced with:

**N**egotiating negative images imposed by 'friends', relatives and social institutions;

**O**vercoming uncertainties such as finance, education, marriage or remarriage;

**P**rotecting their children from low self-esteem;

**A**djusting to a hurting and/or traumatic experience of death, divorce or separation;

**R**esisting using the children as 'spies' between them and the other parent;

**T**emptation to use children as 'sympathetic ears';

**N**eutralizing children's guilt by telling them, 'It was *not* your fault!'

**E**xisting in a society that provides few social supports for their particular situation;

**R**efusing to settle for less than one can achieve.

## Never enough energy!

Reserve time for the really important things – laughter, love and sharing.

* ***Be lavish with your praise and affection.*** 'Don't keep on scolding and nagging your children, making them angry and resentful' (Ephesians 6:4). Children have a way of living up to our expectations, good or bad. I always liked how my pastor friend, Fred Mapp, would refer to his little children as angels. I started to do that. His actually turned out to be angels. Ours . . . did too!

Children need praise and encouragement.

* ***Give your children their own space and respect their privacy.*** One day, at the age of twelve, our daughter Kristle was very upset that we had moved her cassette recorder from her room into our room to listen to some music. She fumed, 'But you didn't ask me!' We thought she was being melodramatic. We thought it such a trivial thing, but there are a limited quantity of things and space that our children have control over. Respect them.

* ***Say 'yes' more times than 'no'.*** If we're honest, many times we say no because we're in a hurry or we're preoccupied. If your child makes a request that you think is not in her best interests, for

example chocolate between meals, take time to reason with her. Try to grant small requests, which tell your children their happiness matters. Save your energy for the nuclear explosions.

## Supporting lone parents

**S**end notes and cards; they all say, 'You're remembered';
**O**ffer or help to arrange practical assistance with house maintenance;
**L**isten; don't be quick to give advice;
**O**ffer love, imagination and patience;

**P**ay a visit at weekends and holidays, or when the children are with the 'absent' parent;
**A**sk what is needed, suggest ways of helping, but chat about other things too!;
**R**emember important events and be interested, for example, 'How did the interview go?'
**E**valuate them not as problems, but as people who just happen to be lone parents;
**N**urse parent and children when the parent is ill; there may not be family close by;
**T**elephone calls can be a blessing, especially when you don't do all the talking;
**I**nterest yourself in the life of the children;
**N**ever say, 'Ring when you want something'; most people won't;
**G**ive them a chance to have a night off by being available to babysit.

## Going it alone

Juggling career, family and school can be a struggle for married mothers. And when you're a single parent, the challenge can be even greater. Many single mums find it necessary to move back home or in close proximity to their own mothers for child-care support. At the dawn of 2000, three families in four with children under the age of 18 were being raised by a lone parent, according to the US Bureau of Labour

Juggling career, family and school can be a struggle for married mothers. And when you're a single parent, the challenge can be even greater.

Statistics. Forty three per cent of Black families are female-headed families. Nearly fifty per cent of all children under 18 will, in the next ten years, spend some time in a single-parent household.

Elizabeth Watson has highlighted the following concerns of single parents:

* ***decreased income*** – Black single mothers make less than forty per cent of two-parent households.
* ***increased responsibilities*** – child-rearing, budgeting, home and car care, employment, etc., all carried out by one person.
* ***decreased self-esteem*** – unpreparedness, personal dysfunction, and unrealistic demands that create considerable emotional distress.
* ***increased self-depreciation and doubt*** – lone individuals rarely have sufficient positive affirmation.
* ***poor peer relationships*** – vulnerability to or alienation from significant others are typical behaviours manifested by lone parents.
* ***decreased spirituality*** – we blame God for our problems rather than use life's circumstances to seek a faith relationship with Him.

## An African perspective

Reasons for people being single parents cannot be lumped under one neat umbrella. Some are single by circumstance; others are single by choice. Even then, there may be various underlying motives. Dr Tuntufye Mwamwenda, university dean in South Africa, has identified four causes of single parenting: ✱ shortage of men, ✱ a bleak future, ✱ status and ✱ success. Descendants of Africa cannot ignore the daily reality of the effects of slavery, that institution which, like apartheid, has been denounced by people of goodwill the world over.

Joy Cain wrote, 'Ever since the first slave ship unloaded its human cargo on these shores, African-American families have been in a state of flux. Slavery separated husband from wife, father from son and grandparent from grandchild in the cruellest, most inhumane way imaginable – so much so that, more than a century after it was abolished, we're still reeling in its wake and trying to overcome racism's present-day strains on our families' – Joy Cain, *Solo Moms*.

## Practical help for single parents

Being a single parent is a challenge. Being a single parent in the midst of a crisis can be nearly overwhelming. Norma Sahlin suggests that church community centres should be equipped with the following:

***Child care facilities.*** Assessing client needs can be stressful, especially if a restless child is present. To enable the visit to run more smoothly, create a child care room. Decorate it with colourful graphics and stock it with safe toys, Christian books and videos.

***Stress management.*** Teach staff members simple techniques of stress control and have a brochure available on managing stress.

***Monitoring for abuse.*** A sad fact of stressful life is that frustrations may be vented in physical and/or mental abuse. All staff members should be taught how to recognize signs of abuse and how to respond.

***Managing finances.*** When facing uncertain income, single parents are in a difficult situation. Money management skills can be shared through pamphlets or a seminar.

***Tutoring.*** Consider setting up a tutoring programme that will help the parent qualify for better employment opportunities. For parents and children, proficiency in reading, writing and computing is essential today.

***Grandparent hotline.*** Recapture the sense of an extended family by starting a grandparent hotline where an experienced person can listen in a non-threatening way and provide assurance, suggestions and referrals.

***Strategies for coping.*** Workshops by single parents for single parents can be a real service to the community. 'Parents' Time Out' is where a group of parents agree to rotate childminding duties so that each has time for rejuvenation and running errands.

***Invite groups to use your centre.*** You don't have to do all the programme planning. Consider offering the use of your centre for little or no charge, but be careful to check out the group's philosophy before allowing them to use your building.

At the Willow Creek Church near Chicago, qualified mechanics fix up cars donated by members and give them to single parents in need. At the Apple Creek Church in Toronto, qualified mechanics from the Men's Organization provide free labour to service the cars of single mothers and carry out repairs.

## Save the children

Singer Marvin Gaye was tragically gunned down by his father in a family dispute. Ironically, the song that he gave to the world was entitled, 'Save the children.' Many children have become caught in the crossfire between two estranged adults. The wounded shoot the wounded using the child as the weapon. What the parents do not realize is that whenever a weapon is fired, the ammunition destroys more than its target. *In the process, the ammunition itself is destroyed.*

## Couldn't you?

'I looked at you and smiled the other day, I thought you'd see me – but you didn't.

'I said, "I love you" and waited to hear what you would say, I thought you'd hear me – but you didn't.

'I asked you to come outside and play ball with me, I thought you'd follow me – but you didn't.

'I drew a picture just for you to see, I thought you'd save it – but you didn't.

'I made a fort for us back in the woods, I thought you'd camp with me – but you didn't.

'I found some worms 'n such for fishing if we could, I thought you'd want to – but you didn't.

'I needed you just to talk to, my thoughts to share, I thought you'd want to – but you didn't.

'I told you about the game hoping you'd be there, I thought you'd surely come – but you didn't.

'I asked you to share my youth with me, I thought you'd want to – but you couldn't.

'My country called me to war, you asked me to come home safely – *but I didn't!'*

Stan Gebhardt

We must save the children. They are worth more than that. Jesus said, 'If any of you causes one of these little ones who trusts in me to lose his faith, it would be better for you to have a rock tied to your neck and be thrown into the sea' (Matthew 18:6). Our children need from us acceptance, activity, and accountability. Jesus died for them. He wants us to love them like He does.

### Acceptance

Children of all backgrounds get into trouble – *not just children of single parents*. We have the choice whether to recoil in horror when we hear of the trouble – or be proactive. A group of about twenty concerned Latino mothers gather every Friday – typically one of the most violent nights of the week – at the Dolores Mission parish in Los Angeles to pray. The women regularly ask themselves, 'What would Jesus do?' After prayer, they follow up on what they believe is an answer to the question.

Children are worth saving. Their future depends on our attitude towards them now.

The group, with bullets sometimes flying overhead, walk through their children's turf carrying signs that read 'We love you' and 'Don't Kill Each Other'. They invite whoever they find on the streets to their next barbecue for the youth of the barrio (Spanish quarter). Greg Boyle, a priest at the Dolores Mission, has buried thirty-two teenage victims of violence. He says, 'If we are going to be the church of Jesus, we have to extend the welcome mat to them.' While it's easy to hate the sin, I believe it takes a power outside ourselves to enable us to love the sinner.

## Activity

The work of our single parents would be so much lighter if it were shared by a community of caring people who provided meaningful activities for their children. One church has its doors open all day and allows its young people to get involved in youth-to-youth activities such as drug awareness and health awareness programmes taken to schools, hospital visitations, prison ministry and mentoring.

One late-night recreation programme in Cincinnati, Ohio, resulted in a twenty-four per cent drop in crime. It was built on the premise that playing basketball is a better outlet for youthful energies than gang-fighting or drug-dealing. We must all get involved – night-time is often a battleground for today's youth. As Norman Gardner, chairman of the Toronto Police Services Board, said in a public forum on teen violence in the Jewish community: 'When a fire is burning, everyone is responsible for helping save the victims.'

## Keys for successful single parenting

* *positive thinking.* We are the barometers of our homes. Our children take their cues from us.
* *setting reasonable and workable goals.* Making lists of daily tasks and activities, tackling what is in your realm to do.
* *giving much love and little criticism to your children, others, and yourself.*
* *accepting praise and giving compliments, again, to your children, others, and yourself.*
* *being patient with yourself and not giving up.* One discouraging day does not erase all your constructive attempts at management.
* *praying without ceasing.* Ellen White writes: 'Keep your wants, your joys, your sorrows, your cares, and your fears before God. You cannot burden Him; you cannot weary Him. . . . His heart of love is touched by our sorrows and even by our utterances of them' – *Steps to Christ,* page 100.

Elizabeth Watson, 'Payoff for the Single Parent', *Message.*

## Accountability

We all need somebody. When God said in Genesis 2:18, ' "It isn't good for man to be alone," ' He wasn't saying we all need to be married, He was saying we all need *somebody.* We all know that everybody is not going to get married but, still, God created us for companionship. Jesus had Peter, James and John. Paul had Mark, Luke and Timothy. We need someone we can offload on, someone we can share with, and someone who can let us know when we're getting off track. Our children need mentors – and so do we. Single parent, be sure you are part of a small, safe group where you can be vulnerable, free to laugh or cry, a group from which you leave strengthened, not drained.

Everybody needs somebody; somebody they can laugh, cry and share with on an intimate level.

One night, a well-known singer was advertised to perform at the Grand Opera House in Paris. That night, the concert hall was packed. Suddenly, the manager went on stage and announced, 'Ladies and gentlemen, I regret that, due to illness, our special guest will not be able to perform this evening. We have found another singer, however, of equal talent, so would you please give her a warm welcome.'

The crowd groaned so loudly that nobody even heard the singer's name. The disappointment could be felt on all sides. The stand-in singer gave it everything she had and, when it was all over, she received brief, scattered applause, followed by uncomfortable silence.

Suddenly, from the balcony, a young girl stood up and shouted, 'Mummy, I think you're wonderful!' Realizing what had happened, the crowd jumped to their feet and gave the girl's mother a standing ovation that lasted for several minutes.

Single parent, you need to be in a group that, every now and then, says to you, 'I think you're wonderful.'

## Well-adjusted

'Please call – urgent. I'm in my room.' That was the message single-parent Elizabeth

Watson got. She dialled the number. Her son was more than 600 miles away. What could be the problem? In less time than it takes to dial eleven numbers, she imagined all kinds of ills and misfortune. In a few seconds she heard his voice.

'I'm not homesick,' he said. 'I just miss our talks. Thanks, Mom, for letting me make my own decisions.'

Elizabeth was both relieved and encouraged. 'When my marriage dissolved,' she said, 'and it became apparent I would be rearing my three children alone, I wondered what would become of us. I could only hope and pray to rise to the responsibility of parenting them alone. My prayers, of course, were for a wholesome family life that would provide well-adjusted people. Now I am realizing this goal, and I am reaping the fruits of my labours. And I can rejoice.'

## Walk the rest of the way

The story is told about three men who were sent on a very important mission. The first man didn't make it because his horse broke a leg. The second man didn't make it because he was ambushed and was wounded in the neck. The third man arrived late, covered in blood. He apologized for the delay, saying in his defence only that it had taken him longer than he'd hoped because he'd been captured and hurt, and as he'd lost his horse he had no choice but to walk the rest of the way.

Single parent, some of you have lost your horse, your source of livelihood; for some of you, your hopes have been ambushed, for others your heart has been wounded. Take a look at your children – you have no choice. Walk the rest of the way. And hear God saying, 'Fear not; you will no longer live in shame. The shame of your youth and the sorrows of widowhood will be remembered no more, for your Creator will be your "husband". The Lord of heaven's armies is his name; he is your Redeemer, the Holy One of Israel, the God of all the earth. For the Lord has called you back from your grief – a young wife abandoned by her husband. For a brief moment I abandoned you. But with great compassion I will gather you' – Isaiah 54:4-7.

# Solowork on Chapter 7

## Falling, hiding or climbing?

Put your own interpretation on the figures below. Some are climbing up by themselves or with the help of others. Some are building themselves a secure platform. Some are falling. Some are burying their heads in the sand. Some are even sawing the tree branch that's supporting someone else. Where do you see yourself? *If you're not satisfied with that position, what are you going to do about it?*

## READ ON!

| Author | Book title | Publisher |
|---|---|---|
| Johnson, Jeanette | Survival Tips for a Single Parent | Review & Herald |
| Henshall, Steve Ann | Is This a Daddy Sunday? Healing the Scars of Divorce | Monarch |
| Jakes, T. D. | Help! I'm Raising My Children Alone | Creation House |

# Chapter 8

# Have you seen her?

Dear Diary

One day when I went to visit Bob in the hospital, I felt there had been a change in his attitude. He seemed scared. He tried to act and talk naturally but suddenly he burst into tears. 'I'm dying,' he said. 'I overheard one of the doctors telling his students, "That was a typical case of Hodgkin's disease – no known cure . . . ." What a horrible way for him to have found out, I thought. Now he wondered what else we were hiding.

When I saw how weak and unhappy Bob was, my heart broke. My mind knew that my love should be strong enough to wish him the best possible way out. I knew I should ask God to take Bob quickly and painlessly if He did not mean for Bob to get well. I couldn't do it. I just couldn't. Instead I kept praying, 'Please don't take Bob from me. I need him so much. I'm not brave enough or strong enough to say, "Thy will be done." Please, dear God, let Bob live. I need him so terribly.'

April 27 was Bob's thirty-fifth birthday. We had been told by the doctor that Bob would probably never see his thirty-sixth birthday, and yet, when he blew out all the candles, both he and I burst into tears from utter relief. I was so sure that this was a sign that a 'miracle' would happen.

I had gone home to do some grocery shopping and received a message that I'd better come back to the hospital right away. I probably broke every speed law getting back to the hospital. I went over to the bed. Bob took my hand and told me that I was beautiful, and said he wanted to apologize; he was sorry for nagging me about my weight and asked me to forgive him.

He kissed me, really kissed me as he had been too weak to do in months, and said, 'That ought to keep you for a while.' By 2.45 Bob had gone into a state of shock. He was trembling from head to foot. I said every prayer I could think of, but mostly the Twenty-third Psalm: 'Yea, though I walk through the valley of the shadow of death, I will fear no evil. . . .' At 3.40 in the afternoon, Bob was officially dead.

The past ten months were the hardest months any of us will probably have to face. I feel sorry for Gail. She had her sixth birthday a week later with no Daddy. Linda was fourteen months on the day her father died. She'll never remember him. And I? I must be a wife to no husband, a mother to two fatherless babies. I must learn self sufficiency and independence – but how? And how do I fill the empty void that stretches as far as I can see?

From the diary of Edna Stone, aged 30.

## Assumptions

The story is told of the father who found his son in bed when he should have been at school. The father spoke to his son and hoped it would not happen again. It did; the very next day – and the day after. Finally, in desperation, the father asked the son to give him three reasons why he should not go to school. 'Well, firstly,' said the son, 'firstly, school is boring. Secondly, the children bully me. And thirdly, I hate the teachers.' The father said, 'Now I'll give you three reasons why you *should* go to school. Firstly, it's your duty. Secondly, you're 45 years old. And thirdly, after all, you are the principal!'

Things are not always what they seem. How often we assume things. How often we assume a bereaved spouse is doing well, just because he or she is looking as well dressed as usual. Like the principal, there are days when just getting out of bed takes every ounce of strength that you have. Paul Tillich wrote, 'Short is the time between birth and death – and it seems so long.' Ellen White wrote, 'The human family have scarcely begun to live when they begin to die.' – *Christ's Object Lessons,* page 342. And nothing can compare to the death of your spouse.

C. S. Lewis wrote in *A Grief Observed,* 'No one ever told me that grief felt so like fear. I am not afraid but the sensation is like being afraid. The same fluttering in the stomach, the same restlessness, the yawning. I keep on swallowing. At other times it is like being mildly drunk, or concussed. There is a sort of invisible blanket between the world and me. I find it hard to take in what anybody says. Or, perhaps, hard to want to take it in. I dread the moment when the house is empty. If only they would talk to one another and not to me.' And the question is asked repeatedly but futilely, Have you seen her? Have you seen her?

Pastor David LeRoy McCottry – he was *our* pastor. As young people we listened to him. We looked up to him. We loved him. He married us. One day we heard the news: he was found dead in tragic circumstances. When I consider what our pain was like, I can only faintly begin to comprehend what his wife and children, parents, siblings and extended family experienced.

As we search for a scapegoat, someone responsible for the death, all we can find to say are the words of Jesus' parable of the man who planted wheat and discovered weeds: 'An enemy hath done this' (Matthew 13:28, KJV).

Losing someone close involves a lot of different emotions and questions. Death is the enemy but Jesus Christ is the hope.

Denika was desperately trying to save all her pennies so that she could buy a doll and a pram. She collected empty bottles and returned them to the shops, she did odd jobs around the house, anything to earn money.

One night, her mother overheard her praying: 'O Lord, please help me to save all my money for that doll and pram. The doll is so beautiful and I know she would be very happy with me. If I get them, I promise I'll let my friends play with them too.'

Denika's mother felt very proud of her daughter. But just when she thought the prayer was over, Denika added these words: 'And please, dear God, don't let the ice cream man come down our street this week!'

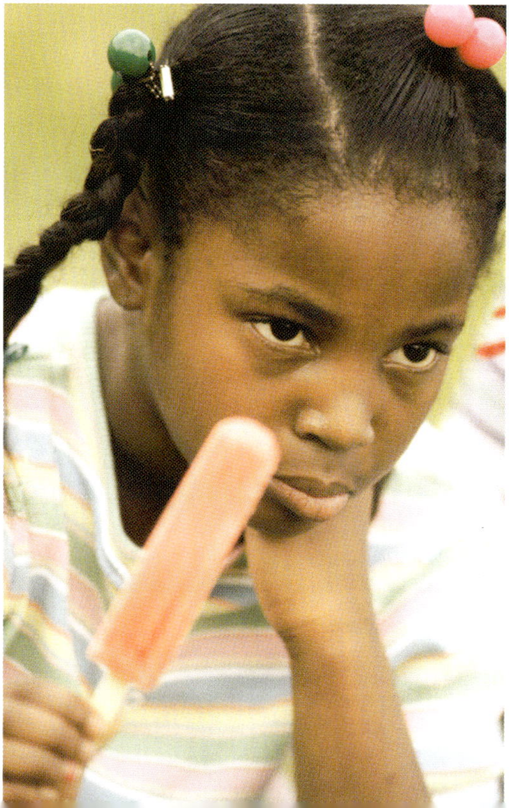

Children make us smile, don't they? But let me give you something you can count on: as sure as Satan is called 'the tempter', he will come down your street this week. And as sure as Satan is the enemy, sorrow and heartache will find their way to your house.

In the Bible, Jonathan knew he might never see David again, and he said, ' "You will be missed, because your seat will be empty" ' (1 Samuel 20:18, NKJV). The reality of death is the reality of the empty seat.

## The empty seat

There's an empty seat at the dining table. There's an empty seat on the sofa. There's an empty seat in the car. There's an empty seat in the bedroom. Birthdays will now be difficult. So will anniversaries and holidays. You go through all of the stages: disbelief, denial, blame, guilt and ultimately, with God, to acceptance and growth. You hear people ask, 'How is she coping?' I don't think God ever expects us to cope with death, because it was never part of His plan.

The Bible actually refers to it as the enemy; but talk about it. People may feel awful and you may feel awkward, but you can try saying, 'Would you mind if I talked a little about Jim.' Once you have broken the ice, it will be easier next time.

The shock can last a few days. Then comes a measure of control, through until the funeral proceedings. Then don't be surprised if you experience a period of

## Those first few months – Dos and don'ts

**Do** accept help from others if it is offered and ask outright for any help you need.

**Don't** bottle up your feelings or feel ashamed of showing them.

**Do** expect to have good and bad days.

**Don't** dwell on all the things you feel you should have said or done.

**Do** try to keep life as normal as possible, especially for any children in the family.

**Don't** think you should be 'over it' by now.

**Do** seek a bereavement specialist if you have no one close to talk things through with.

**Don't** make any major changes in the first year, for example, moving house.

**Do** give yourself time to adjust to your new circumstances before adding even more stress.

**Do** look after your health.

regression, before arriving at some measure of adaptation. There is a broad range of feelings and behaviours that are common after a loss.

## The empty nest

This is a term usually reserved for that period in life when children leave home and couples look at each other and wonder what they will now talk about. When your husband or wife has gone – the one with whom you've shared a bed for twenty years and more – that's when the nest is really empty. A funeral is always an ordeal, but it is also the start of coming to terms with death. It will certainly help to add a personal touch to the service, such as a reading, special music or a special poem.

In the west, you hear it said, 'Leave them alone to grieve.' No, *don't* leave them alone! Grief is not private. When his friend was killed in battle, David said, 'How I weep for you, my brother Jonathan; how much I loved you!' (2 Samuel 1:26).

### Making the funeral special

'I've always regretted that at my mother's funeral, we booked a priest who'd never met my mother, pronounced her name incorrectly, and made general remarks about how nice she must have been,' one woman said. 'When my dad died, I was determined not to make the same mistake. I wrote a special tribute about all the things my dad had achieved, where he'd worked and some of the hilarious things he did and asked the pastor to read it. It made the service very personal and special and I think it helped me get over his death more quickly.'

## Phases of mourning

Period of numbness
Period of yearning
Period of disorganization and despair
Reorganized behaviour

## Tasks of mourning

Accept the reality of loss
Accept the pain of loss
Adjust to an environment where the deceased is missing
Withdraw emotional energy and reinvest in new relationships

## Feelings

Sadness. Anger. Guilt and Self-reproach. Anxiety. Loneliness. Fatigue. Helplessness. Shock. Yearning. Emancipation. Relief. Numbness.

## Physical sensations

Hollowness in the stomach. Tightness in the chest and throat. Over-sensitivity to noise. A sense of depersonalization. Breathlessness. Weakness in the muscles. Lack of energy. Dry mouth.

## Behaviours

Sleep disturbances. Appetite disturbance. Absent-mindedness. Social withdrawal. Dreams of the deceased. Avoiding reminders of the deceased. Searching and calling out. Sighing. Crying. Restless over-activity. Visiting and carrying objects of the deceased.

So don't be afraid to show emotion and affection. And even if many people are there, the bereaved will appreciate *your* presence. Don't worry what to say; go to listen. Let the bereaved talk about his or her loss.

You'll probably feel helpless – that'll be just fine. This is not the time to have all the answers. You might consider writing a letter, or designing your own sympathy card. You could send a little gift as an expression of your concern. From time to time, keep in touch by phone. Be observant of jobs that need doing.

See if you can arrange for someone to look after the children, if there are any. A lone parent needs to be able to enjoy adult company. Above all, continue to be a cheerleader. Let her know, let him know, that together you're going to make it, because if one member suffers, we all suffer together (See 1 Corinthians 12:26).

By making yourself aware of your single-parent friend's needs you can be a truly supportive friend.

## 'I felt I'd died too . . .'

Every two hours, someone in Britain takes his or her own life. For relatives and friends left behind, the legacy of suicide can be an unbearable burden. One April, Clarice, a school teacher, returned home from work to find that Roy, her husband of twenty-four years, had gassed himself with car fumes in the garage of their house.

Clarice battled with feelings of guilt, anger and despair. She felt isolated and lonely in her grief. Although Roy had been depressed, Clarice, 58, had no idea he'd been contemplating suicide. 'I did not know how to get through the days after Roy died. He was my whole life and now he was gone.

'Whenever I mentioned Roy's name in conversation, most people would change the subject because they couldn't cope with what had happened,' she recalls. 'Friends at church tried to help, but they couldn't – I was so deep in despair.' Her doctor suggested counselling. But before the slow and painful path to recovery began, she hit rock bottom.

On the day of her silver anniversary, four months after Roy died, Clarice took an overdose of paracetamol. 'I felt that there was nothing left for me. I felt I'd died too.'

Clarice now works for a bereavement counselling agency. Rekindling her enthusiasm for travelling, she took a holiday to Canada. 'After Roy died, I felt guilty about doing anything – even breathing – because he wasn't there to share the experience with me,' she explained, 'but now my life is very full.'

Fiona Cumberpatch, *Living in the Shadow of Suicide.*

But there's something even more certain than the empty seat and the empty nest – *it's the empty tomb!*

## The empty tomb

There is an empty tomb! Jesus has risen! Death is *not* the end! The Bible says, 'The fact is that Christ actually did rise from the dead, and has become the first of millions who will come back to life again some day' (1 Corinthians 15:20).

Attachment, separation, loss and grief – for men and for women, whether in marriage or not, this is the pattern of life.

The rhythm is inevitable and the course is predictable. What we expect is that we'll marry, live until we're old, and then one of us will bury the other, and comfort ourselves in the hope of the resurrection.

We think that death – when it comes – will come at the right time and with the right amount of warning. The truth is that there will be multiple occurrences of attachment separation, loss and grief. It won't just happen once and you won't always get a warning.

## The joy of sorrow

I have loved
It was beauty.
I have lost
It was hell
I have survived
It was growth
I have recovered
It is heaven.

Mary Joe Hannaford

## When widows and widowers remarry

The divorce rate for widows and widowers who remarry is significantly lower than that of divorced persons. Unlike others who are marrying for the second time, your marriage did not fail. Often the same loving qualities from the first marriage are brought into the second. One remarried father said his children had no difficulty accepting his new wife. 'The fact that their own mother is dead has made it easier,' he said. 'They loved their mother, but she's gone. They don't have to choose.'

Although there are many happily-ever-after stories about widowed people who marry again, one of the commonest problems is the impossibility of living up to the memory of a person who has been idealized in death. As one second wife said, 'He's still in love with his dead wife. How can I compete with a perfect memory?'

In their book, *Real Life Marriage,* Lucy and Dennis Guernsey say, 'Life in the sense of bonding and attachment, death in the sense of despair and hopelessness, burial in the sense of loss and grief, and

### When the news breaks

**PHYSICAL REACTIONS**
- Heart attacks
- Breakdowns
- Insomnia
- Loss of appetite
- Anxiety/Panic attacks

**EMOTIONAL REACTIONS**
- Panic, rage, regression
- Mood swings
- Re-activation of other unresolved losses
- Deep sadness
- Helplessness v. vengeance

**EXTERNAL LOSSES**
- Home
- Extended family support
- Social network

**INTERNAL LOSSES**
- Loss of self-identity
- Loss of optimism/hope/vision for future

resurrection in the sense of renewal and hope are normal in the course of a marriage. There *must* be death and burial as well as life and resurrection. Real life demands it all.'

God in His infinite wisdom has ordained that some things must take place. These we call His *divine necessities.*

## The *must* of tribulation

Firstly, there comes to all of us the *must* of tribulation. The Bible says, 'We *must* through much tribulation enter into the kingdom of God' (Acts 14:22, KJV, italics ours). No one is exempt. Pain and sorrow mar the lives of saints and sinners, losers and winners. All our paths have been strewn at one time or other with the wild weeds of weeping, for there is an unquestionable certainty about suffering.

Jesus said, ' "It is impossible but that offences will come" ' (Luke 17:1, KJV). There is the must of tribulation. Two facts remain: death is inevitable and death is inescapable. The Bible says, 'It is appointed unto men once to die, but after this the judgement' (Hebrews 9:27, KJV). From the very first cry of infancy to the very last cry of old age, we live with death. It stalks us, it stays with us, it finds us, it is inescapable.

Western society does not want to face the fact that every human being is moving unavoidably towards death. And that's *our* death I'm speaking about. Paul Tillich said, 'Do not deceive yourself about the seriousness of death – not death in general, not the death of somebody else, but your own death – by nice arguments for the immortality of the soul. The Christian message is more realistic than those arguments. It knows that we, *really we,* have to die. It is not just a part of us that has to die.'

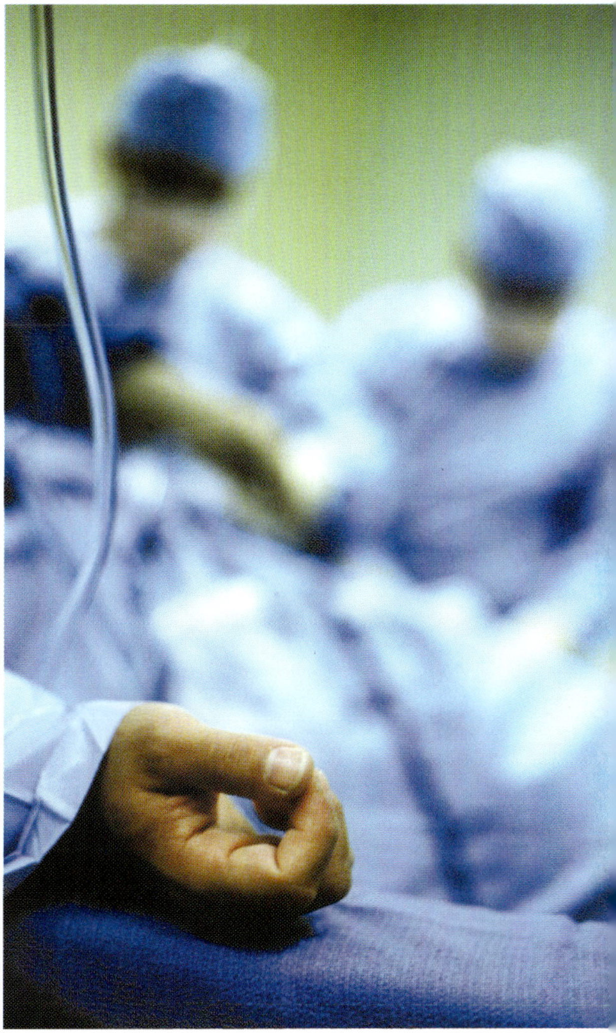

You could be a lifeline to someone in need.

## Pass me not . . .

Pass me not, O gentle Saviour,
Hear my humble cry;
While on others Thou art calling,
Do not pass me by.

Thou the spring of all my comfort,
More than life for me;
Whom have I on earth beside Thee?
Whom in heaven but Thee?

Saviour, Saviour,
Hear my humble cry,
While on others Thou art calling,
Do not pass me by.

Fanny Crosby

But while there may be similarities in how tribulation strikes us, there are differences in how we respond. Some grieve and overcome. Others grieve and succumb. The Christian knows that while she doesn't understand the pain, she can still believe that God is in control.

Oh, she grieves, she hurts just as much as anyone, and God seems so far away. She gropes in the darkness and cries out with Job, 'Oh that I knew where I might find him that I might come even to his seat!' (Job 23:3, KJV).

There is the must of tribulation that leads to a feeling of aloneness and separation, but the Christian draws on unknown resources of faith and rises up to declare with the psalmist, 'Though my father and my mother forsake me, the Lord will take me into his care' (Psalm 27:10, NEB)

The must of tribulation may lead to death, but the Christian's faith somehow soars on eagle's wings. What we celebrate is not the denial of death but the *defeat of death!* It is this that allows us to look death in the eye and cry out, 'O death, where is thy sting? O grave where is thy victory?' (1 Corinthians 15:55, KJV). So in the midst of our pain, our hearts resonate with words of Jesus, 'In the world ye shall have tribulation: but be of good cheer; I have overcome the world' (John 16:33, KJV). But there is a second divine necessity. . . .

## The *must* of salvation

There is the *must* of salvation. The Bible says that God raised Jesus from the dead, therefore, 'Neither is there salvation in any other: for there is none other name under heaven given among men, whereby we *must* be saved' (Acts 4:12, KJV, italics ours). There is the must of salvation. This is the assurance that whether we live or whether we die, our 'life is hid with Christ in God' (Colossians 3:3, KJV). It is the knowledge that 'whoever has God's Son has life; whoever does not have his Son, does not have life' (1 John 5:11).

There is the must of salvation, the divine necessity which says that God 'has given us eternal life, and that this life is in his Son' (1 John 5:11). It is a wonderful thing to be a Christian. It is a wonderful thing, instead of holding my head and saying, 'Good lord, it's morning,' I can wake up, look up to the heavens and say, 'Good morning, Lord.'

## No more separation

'Who then can ever keep Christ's love from us? When we have trouble or calamity, when we are hunted down or destroyed, is it because he doesn't love us anymore? And if we are hungry, or penniless, or in danger, or threatened with death, has God deserted us? No, for the Scriptures tell us that for his sake we must be ready to face

### These three remain . . .

**F**ace the fact that an era has ended; you can never go back.
**A**llow yourself to weep freely.
**I**f you are unwell in any way, check that your heart is not full of bitterness.
**T**ake a firm grip on your finances.
**H**elp God to help others meet your single-parent needs.

**H**elp and serve other people; you need to stay in touch.
**O**vercoming grief is a mark, not of callousness, but of courage.
**P**lan time for rest and enjoyment.
**E**xpress thanks, verbally or in writing, to those who have supported you.

**L**ife is God's gift to you; maintain your will to live.
**O**pen your heart to God not to spiritualists, mediums or faith healers.
**V**iew the body as a way of accepting death and saying goodbye.
**E**xpect to draw strength from God, who loves you.

death at every moment of the day – we are like sheep awaiting slaughter. But despite all this, overwhelming victory is ours through Christ who loved us enough to die for us. For I am convinced that nothing can ever separate us from his love. Death can't, and life can't. The angels won't, and all the powers of hell itself cannot keep God's love away. Our fears for today, our worries about tomorrow, or where we are – high above the sky, or in the deepest ocean – nothing will ever be able to separate us from the love of God demonstrated by our Lord Jesus Christ when he died for us' (Romans 8:35-39).

It is a marvellous thing to know that 'if God be for us, who can be against us?' (Romans 8:31, KJV). No wonder John Powell entitled his book, *Fully Human, Fully Alive* and wrote, 'On your way to our eternal home, enjoy the journey. Let happiness be double in the joyful possession of what you have and in the eager anticipation of what will be.'

There is the must of salvation. Nothing can compare to it. When memories of a loved one flood my soul and dark, dismal clouds of oppression threaten to obscure the Sun of Righteousness, I cry out in anguish of spirit, 'O wretched man that I am! who shall deliver me from the body of this death?' then something within me responds and I can answer with the apostle Paul, 'I thank God through Jesus Christ my Lord.' (See Romans 7:24, 25.)

But there is one more divine necessity. . . .

## The *must* of the resurrection

In the final analysis, there is the must of the resurrection. Speaking of the heartbreak of Jesus' disciples, the Bible says, 'they knew not the scripture, that he *must* rise again from the dead' (John 20:9, KJV). The apostle Paul adds, 'For this corruptible must put on incorruption, and this mortal *must* put on immortality' (1 Corinthians 15:53, KJV).

### The physical relationship ends too

'At last the funeral was over and reality set in. The man I had wanted to spend my whole life with was gone; at the age of 42 I was going to have to build a new life without him. Someone said, "life is what happens to you while you are making other plans."

'The loss of our physical relationship was almost unbearable. As I lay awake, longing to feel his arms around me, I would thank God that I was still a woman, with all a woman's emotions, then firmly I would turn my thoughts to other things until I was able to drift off to sleep.'

Barbara Gaskin, *A Love Lost.*

## Helping children cope with loss

Ralph Waldo Emerson wrote, 'When it comes to death, children are the forgotten people. When it comes to death, we are all children.' Because children react differently to death, the following steps are common tasks for helping children adjust to a loss:

* Review the relationship with the person who has died.
* Become acquainted with mood changes; be able to label and discuss them.
* Work through the fears and hostilities experienced, accepting that temporary hostility is a normal part of grief.
* Express the sorrow and sense of loss.
* Find an acceptable way of relating to the past for the future.
* Talk about guilt feelings. Get them out where they can be seen.
* Find other people and develop new relationships. Eventually remarriage may be right for you, but don't rush it.

'When it comes to death, children are the forgotten people. When it comes to death, we are all children.'

There is the must of the resurrection! Loved ones separated by the cold, cruel, calculating hand of death will be reunited, never again to part; there is the must of the resurrection! Somebody said, 'Man can live forty days without food, about three days without water, about eight minutes without air, but only about one second without hope.'

That's why the Word of God says to us, do 'not be full of sorrow, as those are who have no hope' (1 Thessalonians 4:13). We have this hope which burns within our hearts, hope in the coming of the Lord! I bring you hope today. Reader, there is the must of the resurrection. It's got to happen, it's going to happen.

'The dead in Christ shall rise first: Then we which are alive and remain shall be caught up together with them in the clouds, to meet the Lord in the air: and so shall we ever be with the Lord. Wherefore comfort one another with these words' (1 Thessalonians 4:16-18, KJV).

For those of us whose spouse is alive today, let's recognize that our spouse, like our child, is ours on loan. Let's love her, spoil her, and compliment her. Let's appreciate him, flatter him, and forgive him. For Jesus' sake.

## On Loan

'I'll lend you for a little time
A child of Mine,' He said,
'For you to love the while he lives,
And mourn for when he's dead.
It may be six or seven years
Or twenty-two or three,
But will you, till I call him back,
Take care of him for Me?
He'll bring his charms to gladden you,
And should his stay be brief,
You'll have his lovely memories
As solace for your grief.

'I cannot promise he will stay,
Since all from earth return,
But there are lessons taught down there
I want this child to learn.
I've looked this wide world over
In My search for teachers true,
And from the throngs that crowd life's lanes,
I have selected you;
Now will you give him all your love,
Not think the labour vain,
Nor hate Me when I come to call
and take him back again?'

I fancied that I heard them say,
'Dear Lord, Thy will be done,
For all the joy Thy child shall bring,
The risk of grief we'll run.
We'll shelter him with tenderness,
We'll love him while we may,
And for the happiness we've known,
Forever grateful stay.
But should the good Lord call for him
Much sooner than we planned,
We'll brave the bitter grief that comes
And try to understand.'

Author unknown

# Solowork on Chapter 8

## It's healing time

* Spend some moments looking at the picture below.
* Now read the story of the widow who had no one to care for her and her son in 1 Kings 17:7-16.
* Make a list of what you can learn from this about healing through giving.

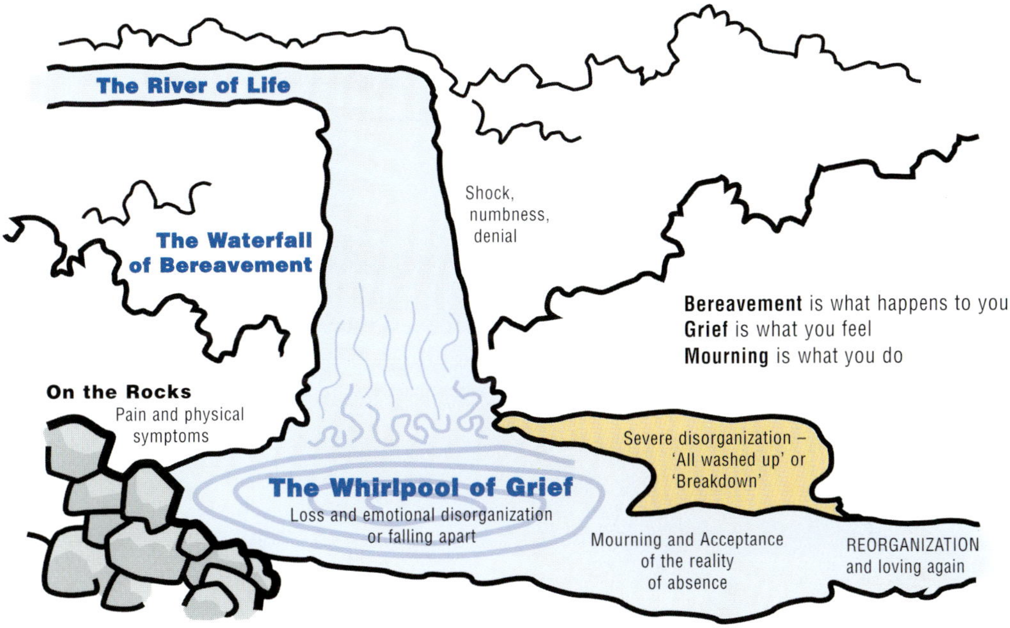


## READ ON!

| Author | Book title | Publisher |
|---|---|---|
| Gaskin, Barbara | A Love Lost: Life After the Death of Your Partner | Harvestime |
| June, Lee N. | The Black Family, Past, Present and Future | Zondervan |
| Mumford, Amy | By Death or Divorce: It Hurts to Lose | Accent Books |

# Chapter 9

# Let's stay together

Dear Dr Brown

We want to thank you for the way you helped to make our wedding day so special. We have been particularly blessed by your sermon at the wedding; the whole day was more than we had prayed for. And we want to encourage you to keep doing what you do!

I must tell you that one of my work colleagues, who is a Hindu, was very inspired by what you said about marriage and how couples should relate to each other. She said that you really made her think about her marriage (which has been a struggle) and the way she treats her husband. She said she has to stop nagging him for all the things done in the past which have resulted in the current financial difficulties they now face. She can see that he has changed for the better, but can't seem to forgive him. When I returned from my honeymoon, she rang me and stated how wonderful your sermon was. When I returned to work she was and still is repeating what you said – what a wonderful witness for the Lord! We had been praying that our wedding day would not only be a blessing to ourselves but to those who attended.

My mother has also been giving positive feedback on how the Holy Spirit has been making an impression on many of the guests who were at the church. For many who have been married some time it has made them look again at themselves and hopefully they are even now making adjustments which will improve their marriage.

Several people also commented about how the whole service was conducted in an organized and spiritual way – indeed, the Holy Spirit was there in our midst. Once again, thank you for allowing the Holy Spirit to use you to bless others who in turn have given God the glory.

We are trying out the 'keys of love' and solicit your continued prayers as our journey together has begun.

Edward and Soneia

Are you putting more effort into keeping your teeth healthy than keeping your marriage healthy?

## Prevention better than cure

Some time ago I received a letter from my dental clinic. It read: 'Dear Mr Brown, It is time for you to have a full dental examination. Your dental team at Rosebank Clinic firmly believe in preventative dentistry. If we are able to prevent gum disease and tooth decay, we can ensure that you have a healthy mouth for life. The system has been fully computerized. We can now offer state of the art dental care, from implants to replacing missing teeth to cosmetic dentistry to restore your smile and confidence. Please telephone the clinic for an appointment.'

I signed up to go to that dental clinic every quarter: spring, summer, autumn and winter. Then I asked myself, Do we invest more energy in preserving our teeth

## Seven stages of marriage – and the common cold

**First year:** 'Sugar, I'm worried about you, my darling. I cannot bear anything to happen to you. I know I'm overreacting but I want you to have a complete hospital check-up and because I don't like hospital food, I'll have yours sent from the Hilton Hotel.'

**Second year:** 'Listen sweetheart, I don't like the sound of that cough. Leave everything. I'll tell the doctor to come and then I'll clear up.'

**Third year:** 'Maybe you'd better lie down, honey, and let me bring you something to eat. Will soup and bread be OK?'

**Fourth year:** 'Look dear, let's be sensible, after you've fed the kids and washed the dishes you'd better hit the sack.'

**Fifth year:** 'What's wrong with you, why don't you just take a couple of aspirin?'

**Sixth year:** 'If you'd just gargle or something instead of sitting around barking like a seal.'

**Seventh year:** 'For heaven's sake, woman, stop sneezing, are you trying to give me pneumonia?'

than in preserving our marriage? I'm not talking now about preventative dentistry for your teeth, but about preventative ministry for your marriage. It's time for all of us to have a full marriage check-up. If we can anticipate the problems then, by the grace of God, it is possible to have a healthy marriage for life.

The Bible says, 'To every thing there is a season' (Ecclesiastes 3:1, KJV). All of us can expect to pass through certain predictable stages in our lives – youth, middle age, late midlife, retirement. These are the seasons of life. And each has its own joys and rewards, its own pressures and pitfalls.

There are four seasons to every year and there are four seasons to every marriage. Ellen G. White wrote a long time ago, 'Our Lord adapts Himself to our special needs' *(Manuscript 51,* 1903). I want to submit to us that no matter what season we are passing through right now, 'in all these things we are more than conquerors through him that loved us' (Romans 8:37, KJV).

## The spring

**Age range 20 – 30** (approximately). I've seen it on college campuses, it's true – love blossoms in the spring! Late twenties is now the most common age for marriage. In 1983 the most common age for marriage was 26 for men and 24 for women. By 1993, it had risen to 29 for men and 27 for women, and it is still going up. The spring of marriage is when the 'bliss factor' is still there. You're still thanking God every day for giving you your spouse.

In the spring, couples are trying to achieve a certain level of economic and educational stability. College, wedding, job. Matriculation, marriage and money – those are the goals of spring! And they are huge goals. Taxing goals. You may have a house loan and a car loan on top of college debts. You're trying to make an impression in your new job. Marriage becomes living to make ends meet. Romance and roses get replaced by bills and budgets.

Wintley Phipps once said that love and marriage were like taking a trip to the moon. Love was like the rocket ride – exciting, exotic, and exhilarating. Marriage, on the other hand, was like the moon – full of cracks, crevices and craters. If we could see what it was like up there before we went – we wouldn't go! And yet being up on the moon, with all those uncertainties and unpredictabilities, relying on your partner and your partner relying on you, recognizing that you need your partner for your own survival, these are the ingredients of which marriage is made. And if you'll just face them with the right perspective, you will discover that they can make you better, not bitter.

You never hear of an astronaut killing his partner, do you? In such close situations you learn about sharing, submitting, listening, negotiating, giving and taking. The world offers you a choice – stay and stagnate or go and grow. The Bible also offers us two options – stay and stagnate or change and commit. Leaving is not an option.

It is the job of premarital counselling to demystify marriage. To serve marriage up in all its reality. Marriage is not about feelings, it's about faith, it is not about contentment it's about commitment. Hollywood supplies an impersonation of

## Waking up – and walking out

'You become used to change and excitement in all other aspects of your life," says Wendy Robinson, a divorced 30-year-old middle manager who works in Manchester. 'When you don't get that from a relationship, there's a problem.'

Wendy's own story is typical. She put pressure on her boyfriend Tim to let her move in with him because she wanted to get married. 'I lived in a frenzy of getting him to name a date,' she says.

Tim was less enthusiastic but they started living together.

After their wedding three years later, things went well for six months. She enjoyed being a Mrs so much that she made sure people on the train could see the ring on her finger. Then, at Christmas, she went to an office party, noticed that the people there looked 'so young, free and single' and suddenly felt miserable. 'It was,' she said, 'like waking up.'

It was also effectively the end of her marriage. *It never, she admitted, occurred to her to try to save it.* Instead she began an affair with another man. Her career and salary gave her independence; the Pill gave her the freedom to be unfaithful; divorce gave her an easy way out.'

what marriage is really like. Watch the end of the movie – the two of them finally fall in love and go off into the sunset. But that's not the end, *it's only the beginning!* Even if you have had frank and open premarital counselling before marriage, recognize that the watchword for the spring is *communication*.

The spring is about getting ready for the race. No one stands on the starting line of Olympic athletics without preparation. When you get married and enter the race of spring, what you are in fact saying is, 'I may pull a muscle in the race, and if so I'll have to deal with it, but I refuse to regret entering the race. I've done all the preparation I can. On your marks, get set, go.'

The spring is the time when you have your first baby, or are thinking seriously about it. Can we afford it? What will it do to my career, our marriage, and my shape? The spring is about waking up to the unexpected and hanging in there during those intensely stressful periods. It is about remembering your priorities, that work is to support the marriage, not marriage to support the work.

Don't overlook your spouse. Don't let other things or hobbies or people take greater priority in your life.

Don't overlook your spouse in the spring. Don't let her question her significance in the whole equation. Recognize that you may struggle at the beginning. Many couples do, only if you ask them, many won't admit it because they genuinely can't remember.

The Bible text for the spring is this: 'For our light affliction, which is but for a moment, worketh for us a far more exceeding and eternal weight of glory' (2 Corinthians 4:17, KJV). When you get through the showers of spring – the hot sun of summer is waiting for you.

## What works for us

Jeanette and Robert Lauer located 351 couples married for 15 years or more and asked them, What are the principal factors which contribute to a lasting marriage? Both partners identified the same choice for the first seven factors:

1) My spouse is my best friend.
2) I like my spouse as a person.
3) Marriage is a long-term commitment.
4) Marriage is sacred.
5) We agree on aims and goals.
6) My spouse has grown more interesting.
7) I want the relationship to succeed.

Other factors agreed upon were:

* We laugh together.
* We agree on a philosophy of life.
* We agree on how and how often to show affection.
* An enduring marriage is important to social stability.
* We have a stimulating exchange of ideas.
* We discuss things calmly.
* We agree about our sex life.
* We share outside hobbies and interests.
* I confide in my spouse.
* I'm proud of my spouse's achievements.

## The summer

**Age range 30-40** (approximately). It is the time of intense activity. Babies are being born. A job promotion is beckoning. The appointment book is getting full as the climb up the ladder of success increases in speed. You have a great deal of energy. You may not hear yourself panting, but you ought to see yourself perspiring. Why are you sweating so much? Because it's summer – the heat is on!

There is so much going on competing for your time. The watchword for the summer is *competition.* Recognize that marriage is a fight. There are no conscientious objectors in this fight. Each partner is a player, either in building the marriage up or breaking the marriage down. Albert Camus said, 'In any fighting group there are those who kill and those who cure. I have chosen to cure, but I still know that I am fighting.'

You will encounter individuals who are competing for what you have. And in the cut-throat world in which we live, some will stop at nothing. They will get their exercise by pushing their luck, running down their friends, jumping to conclusions and hopping mad. Gail Hamilton said, 'The more intimate friends become, whether married or unmarried, the more scrupulously should they strive to repress in themselves everything annoying and to cherish, both in themselves and each other, everything pleasing. I think each should draw on his love to neutralize the

The summer of marriage is the time to realize where your priorities lie. Make time for the children. With so many things and people fighting for your attention don't let the children be the ones who lose out.

faults of their friend; it is suicidal to draw on your friend's love to neutralize your own faults.'

In this fight, children are often the casualties because we do not have time for them. Urie Bronfenbrenner said, 'Our national rhetoric notwithstanding, the actual patterns of life in America are such that children and families come last.' He went on to say, 'Responsibilities to children are to be met, of course, but this is something one is expected to do in one's spare time.'

What you've got to do in this summer season of marriage is, keep all your team on board. Have eyes in the back of your head. Keep one eye on your family life. Keep one eye on your money and careers. Keep one eye on your physical health. And keep one eye on your spiritual health. Take a marriage enrichment inventory.

The Bible text for the summer is this: 'I can do all things *through Christ* which strengtheneth me' (Philippians 4:13, KJV, emphasis ours). When you get through the heat of summer – the 'fall' of autumn is waiting for you.

## The autumn

**Age range 40 – 55** (approximately). This is the time of the year when nature turns brown. Leaves fall off trees and flowers start to wilt. Your grass doesn't grow as much and now the sun sets earlier on those long days of summer which seemed as if they would never end. Life seems more finite now. That pension seems more realistic now. Autumn is known in America as 'the fall'. It is the time when your marriage is most in danger.

The watchword for the autumn is *change*. You're in midlife now. Now is when people feel the need to change – location, job, or even partner. Like Abraham, some seek a better country. We used to have a joke in the seminary that if you got a call to go and work in California, you knew it was from the Lord. In autumn, people feel either they make a move now, or they never will.

What you must realize in this season in particular, is *that the person to whom you are married is not the person you married.* Husband, she has moved on! African American gospel singer Marilyn McCoo says she tells men all the time, 'Women change. We don't start to figure out who we are until our late 30s or early 40s.'

The autumn is a time when we are vulnerable to an affair because we want to preserve the beauty of youth. Husbands wanting to trade their wives in for a newer, younger model. It's not important that your wife be attractive to everyone else, it is important that your wife be attractive to you. If she's overweight, don't fuss, go out walking together or go to the health club with her. And by the way, have you

## Drink from your own well

Drink waters out of thine own cistern, and
Running waters out of thine own well.
Let them be only thine own, and not strangers' with thee.
Let thy fountains be blessed: and
Rejoice with the wife of thy youth.
Let her be as the loving hind and pleasant roe;
Let her breasts satisfy thee at all times; and
Be thou ravished always with her love.
And why wilt thou, my son, be ravished with a strange woman,
And embrace the bosom of a stranger?
For the lips of a strange woman drop as an honeycomb
And her mouth is smoother than oil:
But her end is bitter as wormwood,
Sharp as a twoedged sword.
Her feet go down to death;
Her steps take hold on hell.
Can a man take fire in his bosom and his clothes not be burned?
Can one go upon hot coals, and his feet not be burned?
So he that goeth in to his neighbour's wife;
Whosoever toucheth her shall not be innocent.
Whoso committeth adultery with a woman lacketh understanding;
He that doeth it destroyeth his own soul.
Let thine eyes look right on, and let thine eyelids look straight before thee.
Turn not to the right hand nor to the left:
Remove thy foot from evil.'

*Selected verses from Proverbs 4, 5 and 6 (KJV).*

## Marriage Myths

- Your mate belongs to you.
- You will never be lonely again.
- Your mate will never be attracted to another person.
- All problems in marriage revolve around sex.
- Jealousy means you care.
- You don't love each other if there is conflict between you.
- Sex will be the earth-shaking experience it is supposed to be.
- Each partner will play in marriage the role for which he or she was biologically designed.
- You therefore have a right to expect one thing of a husband and another of a wife.
- Marriage will bring happiness, comfort and security.

looked in the mirror lately and seen what *she's* had to put up with?

A cartoon pictured two fields divided by a fence. Each field had a mule and each mule had his head stuck through the fence, eating the grass from the other mule's pasture. Although each was surrounded by more grass than he could eat, the other field just looked better. In the process, the mules had got their heads caught in the fence and they were braying furiously. The caption under the cartoon read, 'DISCONTENT'. We need to *stop believing the devil's lie that the grass is greener on the other side!* Realize that infidelity is often the result of *an extended period of unresolved resentment*. It is often the result of a crisis, not necessarily the cause of one.

Here's where you need a buddy. A friend. An older person would be extremely helpful. Someone with whom to share your dreams, your frustrations, your fears, and your failings. Autumn is a time of coping with failure and with success. We need to recognize that no person is immune from the autumn. No profession is inoculated from the fall.

Despite what Hollywood will tell you, attraction does not have to be fatal! You can love again! You can rediscover the beauty of your own marriage. Go together on a marriage enrichment weekend or read Dave and Claudia Arp's *The Ultimate Marriage Builder: A Do-It-Yourself Encounter Weekend for you and Your*

*Mate*. It's designed to revitalize your relationship with fun, romance and intimacy.

The Bible text for the autumn is this: 'When he saw the wind boisterous, he was afraid; and beginning to sink, he cried, saying, Lord save me. And immediately Jesus stretched forth his hand, and caught him.' (Matthew 14:30, 31, KJV). A hymn for the autumn would be, 'Change and decay in all around I see. O Thou who changest not, abide with me.' When you get through the fall of autumn – the stillness of winter is waiting for you.

## The winter

**Age range 55 and onwards** (approximately). At its best, winter is a season of new freedom and closeness to God. At worst, winter is a time of despondency and feeling useless. Sometimes it is filled with regret and remorse. You look back over your life and see things you might have done differently, but the clock cannot be turned back. That child that didn't turn out the way you had hoped – what went wrong? The consequences of bad habits, missed opportunities and wrong decisions stare at you every day. But winter is also a time of readjustment and reflection. You see now what really matters in life and you spend time with that.

Many of us are fearful of the winter winds of declining health and dwindling finances. We are saddened by the snows that fall over the graves of our loved ones. Dark comes quickly in winter, oh, yes it does! Your body is not what it used to be. Your mind may not be what it used to be. *But you still have your will.* The will to go on. The will not to give in. The will to keep being productive, to keep giving to someone, to keep the fires of your marriage burning, or to cope with life alone. Don't cave in. You can still be productive. Be a mentor to a younger person. Pass on some of those skills, some of that wisdom that God has given you. Revelation 12:11 says, 'They defeated him by the blood of the Lamb, and by their testimony; for they did not love their lives but laid them down for him.' Three factors are critical to the survival of your marriage: the **life,** the **love** and the **Lamb.**

## The life

Somebody prayed: 'Dear Lord, so far today I've done all right. I haven't gossiped, lost my temper, been nasty, greedy, grumpy, overbearing, selfish or obnoxious. I'm really glad I've accomplished all these things on my own. But in a few minutes, Lord, I'm going to get out of bed – and from that point on, I'll need all the help I can get from you.' Isn't that the reality of our lives?

Before marriage you put forth some effort in order that you will appear attractive to your partner. Well, hear this – *keep up the effort!* For some reason we think that we can show our spouse our real selves now that we're married and our spouse will still be attracted to us.

So you have an argument, he shouts, she cries, and he says to the counsellor, 'That's just the way I am, that's my real self.' Well, we know there's a skeleton there, but we don't want to see it, we want it covered with flesh. In the same way, we don't want to see your real self, we want to see your life covered by the life of

When we are trying to attract a spouse we put tremendous effort into appearing physically attractive. We need to maintain that effort at all stages of marriage.

Jesus! When you accepted Jesus' death, your old self died with Him. We don't want to see it again – neither should you. 'And since your old sin-loving nature "died" with Christ, we know that you will share his new life' (Romans 6:8).

## The love

Chris Spielman played for the National Football League in America. He was known as a tough, no-nonsense player who had an intense love for the game. But when his wife was diagnosed with cancer before the 1998 season began, Spielman chose to miss an entire year of football to take care of her. He told reporters that his decision was based on his love for his family.

'I told Stephanie,' he explained, 'that I want to be the one to take her to treatments. I want to be the one to hold her hand. I want to be the one to take care of my kids when she can't.'

Alan Loy McGinnis tells the story of a woman whose husband had an operation that incapacitated him for customary sexual intercourse. 'Afterward,' says Dr McGinnis, 'he rehearsed a little speech to make to his wife about how he would understand if she decided to get a divorce. But before he could even get started, she said, "Sam, if you're going to get rid of me, you'll have to think up a lot better excuse than this one." Then she told him she'd rather live her life with half of him than with all of any other man. They are still together and, as nearly as I can tell, she is a fulfilled woman.'

When we take that marriage vow and promise to stay together – 'For better, for worse, in sickness and in health' – we must wake up and recognize that *things won't always remain the way they are!* The worse *will* come. And at the bottom of the worse is wondering if you made a mistake. Feeling that you have nothing in common. Wondering if you should have married somebody else.

Marriage is a lifetime journey which you travel together as a couple.

Nancy Kennedy married Barry three months after they met – and then discovered they had nothing in common. There had been an overwhelming physical attraction, and now they stayed together because they had vowed to love each other. They spent the first decade of their marriage pondering the 'if onlys'. Nancy wrote an article entitled, 'Did We Make a Mistake?' This was her conclusion – after twenty-one years:

'Instead of bemoaning a "marriage mistake," I relinquished my ideas of what makes a satisfying marriage and asked God to give me a servant's heart towards Barry. Over time he responded by staying home more and choosing to spend time with me. Sigmund Freud said, "Someday, given enough time, we will look back on our lives and discover the most difficult moments have become most precious to us." My "someday" came about ten years ago when Barry gave me a ring he wore as a child, a gold band with a diamond and ruby chip. He said, "When we first got married, I didn't love you. But I do now."

'Through my tears I confessed my original lack of love and added, "I love you now, too." Did we make a mistake? It doesn't matter anymore. What matters is the love we've found from the God who redeems and makes all things new' – *Marriage Partnership,* Summer 1997.

## The Lamb

John Gottman has identified what he calls *The Seven Principles for Making Marriage Work:*

* Maintain a love map.
* Foster fondness and admiration.
* Turn towards instead of away.
* Accept your partner's influence.
* Solve solvable conflicts.
* Cope with unresolvable conflicts.
* Create shared meaning.

Gottman's research lead him to conclude that the most destructive elements

of a marriage are criticism, contempt, defensiveness and 'stonewalling'. The idea of the love map is for people to be aware of their partner's dreams and fears. With this awareness, couples can navigate roadblocks without creating 'emotional gridlock'. I respect the findings of Dr Gottman's Family Research Laboratory in Seattle, Washington, but there are some things which science can't quantify.

Somebody said, 'To err is human, but to forgive divine'. The 'Love Lab' missed the divine element of forgiveness. That's what the Lamb is all about. John said, ' "Look! There is the Lamb of God who takes away the world's sin!" ' (John 1:29). ' "Father forgive these people" Jesus said, "for they don't know what they are doing" ' (Luke 23:34).

The significance of the Lamb is forgiveness. A couple were celebrating their golden wedding anniversary. Somebody asked the wife, what was their secret? She answered, 'On my wedding day, I decided to make a list of ten of my husband's faults which, for the sake of our marriage, I would *always* overlook. I figured I could live with at least ten!' When she was asked which faults she had written down, she replied, 'I never did get around to listing them. Instead, every time he did something that made me mad, I'd simply say to myself, "Lucky for him, it's one of the ten!"' She got it right. Paul says, 'Love . . . does not hold grudges and will hardly even notice when others do it wrong' (1 Corinthians 13:5).

Lamb power can forgive broken promises, broken dreams, broken hearts, a

## Forgiveness

Decide to forgive
For resentment is negative
Resentment is poisonous
Resentment diminishes
And devours the self.
Be the first to forgive,
To smile and to take the first step,
And you will see the happiness bloom
On the face of your human brother or sister.
Be always the first.
Do not wait for others to forgive
For by forgiving
You become the master of fate
The fashioner of life
The doer of miracles.
To forgive is the highest,
Most beautiful form of love.
In return you will receive
Untold peace and happiness.

Robert Muller

Be a forgiver, don't let problems fester. Forgiveness = freedom.

mistake, a fault, a slip of the memory, a slip in the behaviour – yes, even an affair. Oh, I know this is touchy. Alan Loy McGinnis says in *The Romance Factor,* 'The Scriptures take an unequivocal position: It is always a sin to commit adultery.' But Dr McGinnis goes on to say, 'I know of hundreds of wonderful marriages which were shaken by the "earthquake" of infidelity in the past and today the "wronged" partner is very glad that he or she did not panic unnecessarily. A slip is not necessarily the end of the world. Even if you lose a round in today's highly competitive game of love and sex, it should not be the end of your self-esteem and it need not be the end of your marriage.'

Ernest Hemmingway tells the story of a father and his teenage son who lived in Spain. Their relationship fell apart and the son ran away from home. After some years, the father began a long journey in search of the lost and rebellious son. As a last resort, he put an advert in the Madrid newspaper. The advertisement read simply, 'Dear Paco, Meet me in front of the Madrid newspaper office tomorrow at noon. All is forgiven. I love you.' Paco is a popular Spanish name. The next day, at noon, in front of the Madrid newspaper office, there were 800 Pacos,

Forgiveness is not a feeling – it rises *above* feelings.

all seeking forgiveness . . . .

George Roemisch says in his poem *Forgiveness:* 'Forgiveness is the fragrance of the violet which still clings fast to the heel that crushed it.' It is the one thing that still stands when everything else is fallen. Forgiveness is not forgetting. Forgiveness is not pretending. Forgiveness is not a feeling. Forgiveness is not bringing up the past. Forgiveness is not demanding change before we forgive. Forgiveness is rare because it is hard. Forgiveness is costly and substitutional. That's why it took the life of the Lamb.

Understanding forgiveness is mental health insurance and it is for everyone. Mental health expert Hymers Wilson, Jun, states: 'You may be thinking, I haven't got a problem with anyone – I am at peace with the world. There's nobody out there who has done me wrong whom I need to forgive. All the same, it is important to learn about forgiveness because you have learned that events sometimes take you by surprise. People you think you can trust can stab you in the back. They can hurt you unexpectedly. You need something that you can take now to protect you against the blight of bitterness, the bane of betrayal and the affliction of an unforgiving spirit. Dr Jesus doesn't just have cures. He's in the business of prevention.'

Right now God may be calling you to forgive someone who does not deserve it. And somehow you just can't bring yourself to do it. Agony aunt 'Dear Abby' says, 'Only the brave know how to forgive. A coward never forgives. It is not his nature.' So go ahead, and recall the words of that old hymn, 'There is power, power, wonder-working power, in the precious blood of the Lamb.'

## READ ON!

| Author | Book title | Publisher |
|---|---|---|
| Brown, Jeffrey and Brown, Pattijean | Total Marriage: A Guide to Successful Marriage | Autumn House |
| McManus, Michael | Marriage Savers: Helping Your Friends and Family Stay Married | Zondervan |
| Moeller, Bob | For Better or For Keeps: Renewing Your Marriage in the Tough Times | Multnomah Books |

# Solowork on Chapter 9

## The Sex Test

Sex comes with high expectations – and sometimes great frustrations, often because of the myths that surround the subject. Which of the following statements are truth (**T**) and which are myths (**M**)?

| | T/M |
|---|---|
| Sex should be natural and spontaneous – asking for it spoils it. | |
| Men always want and are ready for sex. | |
| Women must wait for the male to initiate. | |
| Anything other than the missionary position is dirty. | |
| Women expect men to know all about sex. | |
| Men must take charge of and orchestrate sex. | |
| For men, in sex, as elsewhere, it's performance that counts. | |
| A man can always tell when his wife is having an orgasm. | |
| Having sex means having intercourse. | |
| Good sex always ends in intercourse. | |
| For a couple to have sex, the man must have an erection. | |
| People living in warmer climates are more sexually active. | |
| Don't show affection to men because they will want sex. | |
| Good sex means both partners having an orgasm at the same time. | |
| Sex is a purely physical act. | |
| There is something wrong with a man having a lower sex drive than a woman. | |
| Women receive more stimulation from a larger penis than a small one. | |
| In this enlightened 21st century, none of the above myths has had any effect on any of us. | |

# Chapter 10

# Help me make it through the night

Dear Dr Brown

I felt the need to write again as circumstances have changed since my seeing the young man concerned this weekend. He said he didn't think I would be talking to him again. He felt I'd been abrupt with him on the phone when he was apologizing for not turning up to see me. This was a year ago. He obviously wasn't concerned enough to try and call. I invited him to a dinner do for my birthday. His response was basically if he's not busy doing something else he may come. I let him know that if he can make it that's fine, if not that's also fine.

I felt his response was a bit rude, however. I cannot know his mind in this matter. The process has been a painful one. I don't know whether this was God's will or not. I would like to think it wasn't, but this is something of which I'm not certain. Maybe this was the only way for God to bring me to this point, or maybe not; I don't know. But what I do know is that there has been spiritual growth through this ordeal. I didn't get the man, but I have definitely been drawn closer to the Man who died for me.

Thank you for your time and advice.

Mary

## Should I get married?

'There are times, when I hear someone say "Singleness is a gift", that I want to throttle them,' said Dr Hyveth Williams at a Singles Seminar in London. 'It sounded to me like saying appendicitis is a gift, or a

migraine headache is a gift. But I discovered that God's will is that we should be members of one another.'

Somebody is asking the question today, 'Does God want me to get married?' The answer is: *God doesn't mind!* Marriage *is* a gift and, yes, *singleness* is a gift. The apostle Paul says if you marry you have done well. If you choose to remain single you have done well too – and in these difficult days, you may even have made a better choice.

Sin has consequences and so does faithfulness to God. Your single state may be as a result of your sin or your faithfulness, but understand this, God has a standard which He expects us to live up to. If you're single, you must struggle to keep your sexual urges under control. If you've got a homosexual orientation, you must struggle to prevent orientation becoming practice. If you're married, you must struggle to remain sexually faithful to your partner.

## Single but not second

Single people, marriage is beautiful, but stop envying the marrieds. Be thankful for what *you've* got! Somebody said if a woman has not met the right man by the time she's 24, she may be lucky! Never-marrieds, you do not have second-best, the Bible says, 'Every good gift and every perfect gift is from above, and cometh down from the Father of lights' (James 1:17, KJV) *and God doesn't give second-rate gifts!*

In 1 Corinthians 7:7 Paul states a general principal that he repeats elsewhere and that is that every believer receives

gifts from God. The Greek language uses the word *charismata* to refer to these gifts, and *charis* means grace. In Romans 12 Paul traces all gifts back to the grace of God. And gifts don't necessarily spring up overnight.

When you see Paul talking about gifts such as leadership and teaching, you can see these are gifts which are developed over time. When Paul talks about the gift of singleness, understand that *singleness is a gift developed over time.* It is the grace of God that enables you to exercise your gift!

If you are married, Paul says you are to develop that gift. Marriage demands commitment and hard work for it to be a success. Singleness also demands hard work. I don't know how long you're going to be single, but God is looking for returns from His investment in you. If you are 30 now and God sees that at 35 you will get married, God is asking you to *give Him the best you've got for those remaining five years.*

One morning, when the Berlin Wall was still standing, some East Berliners came and dumped a truckload of rubbish on the west side of the wall. Greatly angered, the people thought they would return the favour – then they had a better idea. They filled a truck with canned goods, medicine, clothes and other non-perishable items, then took it over to the east side. They stacked it up neatly beside the wall and put a sign near it which read, 'Each gives what he or she has to give.'

What do you have to give? Are you sour because of how others have treated you? Are you bitter because of how life has

## Give the best you've got

A skilful carpenter was ready to retire. He told his employer-contractor of his plans to leave the house-building business and live a more leisurely life with his wife enjoying his extended family. He would miss the pay cheque, but he needed to retire. They could get by. The contractor was sorry to see his good worker go and asked if he could build just one more house as a personal favour. The carpenter agreed but in time it was easy to see that his heart was not in his work. He resorted to shoddy workmanship and used inferior materials. It was an unfortunate way to end a dedicated career.

When the carpenter finished his work, the employer came, but instead of the customary inspection, he handed the front door key to the carpenter. 'This is your house,' he said. 'It's my gift to you.'

The carpenter was shocked! What a shame! If he had only known he was building his own house, he would have done it differently.

You are the carpenter. Each day you hammer a nail, place a board, or erect a wall. Your attitudes and the choices you make today build the 'house' you live in tomorrow. Build wisely! Work like you don't need the money. Love like you've never been hurt. Dance like nobody is watching.

Anonymous

treated you? Can you still find that something to give to someone else, even though you feel you've been dealt a bad hand? Jesus said, ' "For if you give, you will get. Your gift will return to you in full and overflowing measure, pressed down, shaken together to make room for more, and running over. Whatever measure you use to give – large or small – will be used to measure what is given back to you" ' (Luke 6:38).

## Busy or bury?

The Bible tells the story of a man who went on a long journey and left talents or gifts with his servants. Some were busy using their gifts and were blessed; others buried them and were cursed. So many today are just burying the talent of singleness. They cannot function without a partner on their arm, they are just waiting to exhale. There are so many single people who can't wait to be married and so many

Are you burying the talent of singleness?

mixed up married people who can't wait to be single again. Whether single or married, use the gift you've got!

Understand that God's grace does not eliminate your problems. You'll still have to struggle with loneliness. You're still going to struggle with sexual temptation. But now you will hear God saying to you, 'My grace is sufficient for thee: for my strength is made perfect in weakness.' (2 Corinthians 12:9, KJV). And do you want to know the truth? Fulfilled single people make the best spouses – yes they do!

One of the reasons why many of us don't like singleness is because we have never accepted the grace which God extends so willingly to enrich our present circumstances. We don't accept our present status, even though it may be temporary. All we seem to talk about is the greener grass on the other side. You're single – face it and move on. Some of us need a wake up call not unlike the T-shirt which pictured *The Titanic* and read, 'The boat sank – get over it.'

God gives gifts, but He doesn't give broken gifts. Reader, it may be that He has some unfinished business with you so He's putting your partner on hold while He fixes you up. Don't worship the concept of marriage, worship the *Creator* of marriage!

## Taking charge

How many times have you heard someone who was going through a divorce describe his or her mate as the vile, unfair, vicious perpetrator of all the misery? Once anger or hurt enters the mix, your objectivity will give way to self-preservation. Your best chance to get real control of your life is to stop that thinking right now. Don't try to place accountability somewhere else, or you are going to cripple any efforts you are making toward becoming a winner.

Dr Philip McGraw, *Life Strategies: Doing What Works, Doing What Matters*

You are not just a half something – you are a whole person!

Any time the only thing that motivates you to look good is somebody else, it means you have a problem with your self-esteem. Fix yourself up for you, *you* are important! I am not a broken piece looking for another broken piece to make me whole, I *am* whole!

He's coming back. Yes He is. And the story tells us that when He comes back He will ask the person with ten gifts what he did with them. Then He will address the person with five gifts, and so on. Perhaps you don't see yourself as a ten-talent person or even a two-talent person. If you give your singleness to God, you will possess it as a gift. Margaret Clarkson says in her book, *Single:* 'Touched by God's grace, being single becomes a good thing – even God's best – *for those who choose to seek it in him.'* So you have one gift! Didn't you ever hear about the 'one-note musician'?

## Play your one note

The musician took her seat in the orchestra, arranged her music and tuned her instrument. As the concert began, the conductor skilfully cued one group of musicians, then another until finally the crucial moment arrived. It was time for her note to be played. The conductor signalled her, she sounded her note and the moment was over. The orchestra played on and the 'one-note player' sat there quietly for the rest of the concert, not lamenting her one note but glad that she played it when the conductor asked her!

Reader, I don't know how long you've been single, or single again, and you don't know how long you're going to remain single, but I want you to know in this period of your life in which you are single, you have a gift. Single – ✱ by death, ✱ divorce, ✱ decision, ✱ delay, ✱ single-parent or ✱ spiritually single – one person alone, the message of this book is, *play your one note now!*

Don't put your life on hold looking for someone to partner you. So often we don't see the gifts that God has planted in us. Instead of burying them, invest them.

You've got gifts of listening and sympathy, go and sit with some senior citizen or offer comfort to a mother who's just lost her child. You have a little finance, it's a gift, invest it in life insurance, a pension, property, education, one day it will bear fruit. Somebody is going to be glad they met you, somebody is going to be enriched because they met you, don't look at what you can get from a relationship, prepare yourself for what you can give.

## Hope chest

In Bible days, no one got married without a dowry. A dowry was the price paid by the suitor to the parents of the perspective bride. It was also the portion which the bride brought to her husband. In other words, no one came into the relationship with an empty suitcase. They felt valued and appreciated. They had a whole life when they came into the relationship. When I was courting my wife I would always hear about something called a hope chest. When the time was right I found out what it was and what was in it: linen, towels, table cloths, the best china, silverware, and more! Deuteronomy 28:2-6 says, ' "These are the blessings that will come upon you:

> Blessings in the city,
> Blessings in the field;
> Many children,
> Ample crops,
> Large flocks and herds;
> Blessings of fruit and bread;
> Blessings when you come in,
> Blessings when you go out." '

Reader, your blessings will seek after you while you are seeking after God. Let God find you on your way while you are busy going forward. *God has not forgotten you!* David said, 'The one thing I want from God, the thing I seek most of all, is the privilege of meditating in his Temple, living in his presence every day of my life' (Psalm 27:4). And God says, Because you desired that one thing I'm going to give you other things, 'Seek ye first the kingdom of God, and his righteousness, and all these things shall be added unto you' (Matthew 6:33, KJV).

As a single who is saving themself sexually until marriage, as a single who refuses to accept Hollywood's dating lifestyle and the standard for God's children, you might as well know now, people will make fun of you. You might be in an unhealthy relationship right now and God is telling you to break it off – because He has something better. When you put edification before entertainment, perseverance before pleasure, and commitment before contentment, you will be ridiculed – even persecuted – but you will not be the first. Remember Gethsemane.

## Undistracted devotion

Many years ago, a young communist wrote a letter to his girlfriend. He was breaking off his relationship with her because of his devotion to the Communist cause:

'We communists have a high casualty rate. We're the ones who get shot and hung and ridiculed and fired from our jobs and in every other way made as uncomfortable as possible. A certain percentage of us get killed or imprisoned. We live in virtual poverty. We turn back to the party every penny we make above what is absolutely necessary to keep us alive. We communists do not have the time or the money for many movies or concerts or T-bone steaks or decent homes or new cars. We've been described as fanatics. We are fanatics. Our lives are dominated by one great overshadowing factor, the struggle for world communism. We have a philosophy of life which no amount of money could buy. We have a cause to fight for, a definite purpose in life. If our personal lives seem hard or our egos appear to suffer through subordination to the party, we are adequately compensated by the thought that each of us in his own small way is contributing something new and true and better for mankind. There is one thing in which I am in dead earnest about and that is the communist cause. It is my life, my business, my religion. It is my hobby, my sweetheart, my wife, my mistress, my bread, my meat. I work at it in the daytime and I dream of it at night. Its hold on me grows, not lessens, as time goes on. Therefore, I cannot carry on a relationship with you any longer, no longer a love affair, not even a conversation with others without relating it to this force which drives and guides my life. I've already been in gaol because of my ideals, and, if necessary, I'm ready to go before a firing squad.'

That is having an undistracted devotion to a cause.

*Singleness,* by Chuck Swindoll

## Gethsemane

'I was so impressed by Gethsemane,' writes the author of a book on the Holy Land, 'I forgot to pray, and it was some time before I noticed the behaviour of some of the tourists. They lit their cigarettes, stuck their hands into their pockets and wandered about – as if at home in their own back gardens. Joking and laughing,' he says, 'they heedlessly tried to turn a great sanctuary into a place of relaxation and enjoyment.'

Gethsemane – how does it affect you? That's where Jesus prayed often, but especially before His trial and execution. And in the Garden that night Jesus saw a cup which was there, and an event took place the full significance of which only eternity will reveal.

## It's the night time

Jesus said, 'My soul is exceeding sorrowful even unto death.' Every word carries the emphasis of overwhelming grief. The poet says, 'Gethsemane, can I forget and there Thine anguish see, Thine agony and bloody sweat and not remember Thee?' It was night-time for Jesus. 'Sympathy and solitude are both desirable in severe trials,' writes Godwin. Single people understand that. Jesus needed sympathy, He needed empathy and so He instructed His disciples to remain and keep watch.

What Jesus was really saying was, I'm so filled up with agony and anguish that if I don't get some help from somewhere I'm not going to make it! Single people can understand that. Jesus needed someone to help Him make it through the night. Jesus' cry was, ' "Father! If it is possible, let this cup be taken away from me" ' (Matthew 26:39).

What did Jesus see in that cup? He looked down through the corridors of time and saw the whole human family, singles and marrieds, children and parents, in a

## The gift of suffering

'Time spent in the fog of pain could be God's greatest gift. The next time you are called to suffer, pay attention. It may be the closest you'll ever get to God.'

Max Lucado

crisis that He would have to suffer for. He saw children carrying guns to school and killing teachers because of a bad grade, children killing other children because they don't look like them. He saw neglected children and busy parents. He saw television study instead of Bible study. He saw husbands beating on wives, and wives cheating on husbands. He saw young people wearing the name of Christ jumping from bed to bed with one another. He saw parents crying for their children and children dying for their parents. He saw wives misused and children abused. He saw husbands claiming to be the head of the home but not willing to be the servant that Jesus was. So Jesus asks in the words of the singer,

'Who really cares? To save a world in
despair
Who really cares? Who's willing to try
To save a world that is destined to die?
When I look at the world, it fills me with
sorrow
Little children today, really going to
suffer tomorrow
Oh, what a shame.'

Jesus saw all of this and He cried, ' "Father, if you are willing, please take away this cup of horror from me" ' (Luke 22:42). But I've got good news for you today. Jesus' prayer didn't stop there. He added the words, ' "But I want your will, not mine." ' For this cause, came I into the world and I'm going to see it through! Not only was it the night time, it was also the right time.

## We need each other

'If all members, young and old, male and female, married and unmarried, rejoice and suffer together, this will not damage our homes and families! Instead, it will liberate us from having to carry the entire weight of defining our own personal worth.'

Audrey Johnson

## It's the right time

Galatians 4:4 says when the time was fully come God sent His Son. It was the night time for Jesus but it was also the right time. Jesus said, 'This is why I came, for messed-up Mary, drugged-up David, poor Peter, rich Robert, pretty Pauline and plain Paul. For God so loved the world that He gave His only begotten Son. I came not to condemn the world, but to save it. I have come that you might have life, more abundantly!'

We've got to learn how to turn our problems into promises. We've got to learn to rejoice in the darkness, not just in the light.

## The answer from Jesus

I know that you are hurting, yes, my
eyes behold your tears
I know there are times you wonder if
My presence lingers near
I know it's hard to hold your faith
when shadows shroud the light
I understand the pain of struggling
through this wintry night

I understand your questions and I
know the cross you bear
I lived on earth among you and
endured more than your share
I, too, want sin to end and will soon
effect its fate
For now I ask your trust in Me, and
counsel you to wait

I want to bear your troubles, how my
heart goes out to you
For times like this I offer you My
strength to bring you through
Don't mourn as do some others,
feeling that you cannot cope
See the imprint of the nails... They
are proof that you have hope.

Candace Hurlock

Reader, it may be night time for you now, but I want to declare to you that it's the right time. God's not going to give you more than you can bear. Don't give up. We've got to learn how to turn our problems into promises. We've got to learn to rejoice in the darkness, not just in the light. We've got to learn how to testify

## United we stand

'Deliver me from retirement communities... or any other place that separates people. We need the young and we need the old and the married and the unmarried and the divorced and the sick and the well. We need each other. We all need Jesus, and Jesus needs all of us.'

H. M. S. Richards, Sen.

when we've lost our job, not just when we've found one; I'm talking about the right time. We must learn to thank God for the cross as well as the crown, for if there is no cross-bearing, there'll be no crown-wearing. Michael Korda, author of *Success!* writes, 'Never walk away from failure. On the contrary, study it carefully – for its hidden assets.'

Turn your eyes away from yourself! Jesus needs you. As long as the devil has you focused on your own pain, he knows you won't reach out to others. Jesus still says, 'Help me make it through the night.' Your life must touch somebody.

I was leaving my aunt's house in Kingston, Jamaica. It was Christmas time, and my grandmother was taking me to her house in the country. As we waited for the bus in an area called 'Six Miles' I saw a heavy-laden vehicle approaching. It seemed to have people not only *in* the bus, but *on* the bus as well. Produce and purchases were in abundance and I announced what appeared very obvious to me, 'Gran, the bus is full.'

We cannot live in a modern world as isolated individuals. We must relate positively to those around us. Our lives must touch somebody!

My grandmother replied, 'Full? what!' She proceeded to pull me and push me and the next thing I knew was that I was on the bus. I gazed at my fellow travellers – they were many. I tried foolishly to carve out some space around me. It was then that I felt people watching me. The bus conductress, with hands on her hips, asked, 'What 'appen to you?' I tried to pretend I didn't know who she was talking to. She continued, 'You 'fraid touch people?' I realized from that experience that *our lives must touch somebody!*

As long as there are people suffering, it will always be night time for Jesus. And it will always be the right time for us to help somebody. The pain of this world is Jesus' pain.

As long as there is desperation and deprivation, discrimination and segregation, separation and isolation, homicide and suicide, it will always be night time for Jesus, and Jesus looks to you and me and says, 'Help me make it through the night.' It's the right time to bring light to someone who sits in darkness.

You have God-given gifts and the time is now to use them. You could bring light to someone who sits in the darkness.

## It's the *light* time

The story came out of California. One lazy summer afternoon, Larry Walters, a truck driver, was sitting in a lawn chair in his back garden wishing he could fly. For as long as he could remember, he wanted to

### Together forever

'Can the church promote stable marriages and healthy family life in society without abandoning the non-married and relegating them to the status of second-class citizens? It not only can, but it must. The true *koinonia* of Christ is not only intergenerational but intramural as well. Not only are all parts of the body to function, but they are to function together.'

Ray Anderson and Dennis Guernsey, *On Being Family.*

go up. To be able just to rise right up in the air and see the world going by all around him, oh, this was his dream. Time, money, education and opportunities for pilot training were not his.

So he tied forty-five helium-filled weather balloons to his lawn chair. He then packed a parachute, a CB radio, some drink, some peanut butter sandwiches and a pellet gun to pop some balloons when it was time to come down. Then, whoosh! Instead of going up 100 feet, as he had planned, he was propelled 10,000 feet! He travelled higher and still higher, above the clouds, up, up and away.

He was eventually spotted by a DC10 airline pilot. The pilot radioed in the news to headquarters about the strange sight of a man flying through the air in a lawn chair. The pilot was immediately ordered to land, because they thought he was hallucinating. When the Larry Walters flying machine eventually reached the ground, reporters swarmed around him like flies. One pushed a microphone in his face and shouted above the din of her colleagues.

'Were you scared?' she asked.

'Yep,' replied Walters.

'Would you do it again?' asked the reporter.

'Nope,' he said.

'But what made you do it in the first place.'

Larry paused, thoughtfully scratched his head, looked earnestly into the camera and said, 'Well, you can't just sit there.'

It was Dr Calvin Rock, author of *Go On!,* who stated, 'You can get run over on the right road if you just sit there.' It is not simply the deeds of evil people that cause trouble in our world, it is also the silence of good people, people who can't be bothered to help.

'She was crying, and screaming, and yelling,' say Neil Jacobson and John Gottman in their book *When Men Batter Women,* 'and then – to shut her up, he later told the police – he began to choke her. She couldn't breathe, and she thought he was, in fact, going to kill her.' All over the world there are women trapped in life-threatening marriages. Who will help them make it through their night?

In all the studies done on the misery of

divorce, Polly Toynbee states in the *Guardian,* 'They never assess how many millions have been freed from lives of unspeakable married misery that their ancestors were forced to suffer.'

It was C. S. Lewis who said in *Screwtape Letters,* 'The greatest evil is not done in those sordid "dens of crime" that Dickens loved to paint . . . . It is conceived and moved, seconded, carried and minuted . . . in clean, carpeted, and well-lighted offices, by quiet men with white collars and cut fingernails and smooth-shaven cheeks who do not need to raise their voices.'

It's time to let our light shine. We must speak out against legislation which protects the violator and punishes the victim. Dr Charles Dudley, author of *Thou Who Hast Brought Us,* says, 'We must stand for the rights of the oppressed and neglected. Threats, anger, political risk – nothing should stop us.' Night may descend on Friday, but light can ascend on Sunday.

We may be alone, but we can bring light to someone who sits in darkness. And to those of us who do, Jesus says, 'Inasmuch as ye have done it unto one of the least of these my brethren, ye have done it unto me' (Matthew 25:40, KJV). Dr Martin Luther King, Jun., poses the question, 'Who are the least of these?' He answers, 'They are God's children who wake up every morning standing on tiptoe's stance, not knowing what to expect next, who are the least of these.

Men who use violence on women are violators. We need to speak out against laws that protect violators and punish victims.

'They are the boys and girls who get up every day and have nothing to look forward to because they can't find a job, who are the least of these.

'They are the people who see life as nothing but a long and desolate corridor with no exit signs, who are the least of these.

'They are people who see no hope, no way out, who are the least of these.

'They are people who have been deprived of educational opportunities, who are the least of these.

*'They* are the people at the bottom of the economic ladder.'

And we need to let them know that there is a balm in Gilead!

If it's taking so long for your light to shine because of the sadness of your circumstances, my word for you today is, hold on.

A star will shine.
A child will be born.
The wise will follow.
The shepherds will kneel at the cradle.
The kings will find the manger
The word will become flesh and dwell among us.
The glory of the Lord shall be revealed.

## I have a dream

I have a dream of a nation in which all churches esteem single adults as equal to those who are married. A dream of single people taking their role in leadership at all levels. A dream of great relationships between married and single people, old and young. One where burdens are shared, homes are open and needs are met. A dream where divorcees, single parents, widows and widowers all receive lots of love and support. A dream where single people meet together without gossip of relationships and pressure to pair up. A dream where single people are living holy lives, supporting one another *to shine as lights in the darkness* and avoiding all moral compromise. A dream where Christians of all kinds understand the strategic role that single people can have in Christian service at home and overseas. A dream where those committed to the celibate life are respected, not pitied.

Steve Childcraft, *One of Us*

Every eye shall see Him.
The crooked shall be made straight.
The rough places shall be made plain.
Every knee will bow.
Every tongue will confess.
Justice will well up as waters
And righteousness as a never failing
stream.
Swords will be beaten into
ploughshares
And spears into pruning hooks.
Weeping may endure for a night
But joy will come in the morning.

Trust in God! Trust in God! Trust in God! And I guarantee you, everything will be all right!

## An on-time God

God supplies all our needs. The song says, 'He may not come when you want Him, but He's always right on time.' Singleness is hard. It's a struggle. It involves pain; but keep the pain in perspective by looking at Jesus. 'After all, you have never yet struggled against sin and temptation until you sweat great drops of blood' (Hebrews 12:4). That's why the songwriter said, 'Lest I forget Gethsemane; lest I forget Thine agony; lest I forget Thy love for me; lead me to Calvary.'

Spend your energy working, not waiting. Trust the God who made you to know what you need. God acts when we act. When God hears us thank Him for answering our prayers, even before we have seen the result, God acts. When God sees us laying aside money for Him first and then thanking Him for providing for our bills and groceries, God acts!

The story is told of a woman who went to her cupboard and it was bare. She prayed that God would provide, and then she thanked Him. She said, 'Praise the Lord.' She cried, 'Hallelujah!' Somebody said, you don't have to wait till the battle is over, you can shout now! The problem was that her verbal praise did not go unnoticed by her non-believing neighbour. He was tired of hearing this woman pray and praise. Sometimes he would see her open her front door and skip down the road singing! He said to himself, 'Needs

food from God, does she? Well, I'm going to fix this woman once and for all.'

The man went to the grocery shop. Not just any grocery shop – the best. He filled up with expensive name-brand goods. He returned home, placed the shopping bags on her doorstep and hid behind a tree. Pretty soon, as was her custom, the lady came out of the house with a song on her lips. She looked down and saw the packages, food of every kind, and the best! What do you think she did? She ran down the street and skipped back praising the Lord!

The atheist couldn't take it any more. He leapt from behind the tree. 'Lady, what are you praising God for?' he asked. 'Look!' she replied. 'I had no food and God has supplied all my needs.' *'God* didn't supply all your needs,' said the man angrily. *'I* was the one who bought all those groceries, and they were not cheap either!'

The woman started up again. 'Praise the Lord, hallelujah, thank you, Jesus!' The man had enough. 'What are you praising God for *now*?' The woman said, 'I knew that God would supply all my needs. What I didn't know was that He would make the devil pay for them!'

The devil's day is coming; your day is here. *Carpe diem* – seize the day! Somebody said yesterday is history; tomorrow is mystery; today is a gift – that is why it is called the present. God bless you.

## READ ON!

| Author | Book title | Publisher |
| --- | --- | --- |
| Childcraft, Steve | One of Us: Single People as Part of the Church | Word |
| Richards, Larry | A Healing Gift from God | Word |
| Roberts, J. Deotis | Roots of a Black Future: Family and Church | Westminster Press |

# Solowork on Chapter 10

## Side by side we stand

As you read this book you see the hurts which you have faced and you see the hurts which others have faced. Look at the picture below and ask yourself where is each in relationship to the person in the canoe heading for the falls?

Perhaps the **advice-giver** seems *above* and *far away.* The **reassurer** also seems *above* and at a *distance.* The **understander** is *closer in both dimensions, but* only the **self-revealer** is *on my level* and *very near.*

Your hurts have put you in touch with the hurts of others. The Bible says, 'What a wonderful God we have – he is the Father of our Lord Jesus Christ, the source of every mercy, and the one who so wonderfully comforts and strengthens us in our hardships and trials. And why does he do this? So that when others are troubled, needing our sympathy and encouragement, *we can pass on to them this same help and comfort God has given us'* (2 Corinthians 1:3, 4, emphasis ours). Put your focus on what you are ministering, not on what you are missing.

# Picture credits:

## Stockbyte

1, 3, 5, 6, 10, 12, 13, 18, 21, 48, 58, 59, 63, 71, 73, 78, 79, 80, 97, 98, 99, 102, 107, 130, 136, 137, 140, 141, 143, 147, 148, 153, 154, 162, 164, 165, 166, 168, 169, 170, 172, 177, 179, 183.

## Digital Vision

7, 37, 68, 69, 81, 83, 86, 108, 160, 184.

## Eyewire

7, 16, 19, 40, 42, 43, 44, 47, 49, 52, 58, 65, 72, 96, 108, 111, 112, 113, 120, 122, 124, 126, 127, 128, 129, 134, 135, 142, 145, 154, 167, 189.

## Photodisc

6, 20, 25, 26, 27, 29, 31, 32, 33, 36, 44, 45, 50, 53, 55, 56, 57, 67, 70, 74, 85, 89, 90, 92, 98, 106, 110, 116, 117, 121, 131, 144, 148, 149, 150, 157, 182, 185, 186, 187.

## Corbis Digital Stock

9, 30, 35, 94, 132, 133, 134, 158, 160, 174, 175, 178, 188, 190, cover.

## Corel Images

10, 74.

## Ludwig Werner Binemann

70.

## Stanborough Press

76, 95, 100, 114.

## ITC

181.